Your Ideal Hawaii Move

A Guide for Moving to Hawaii Island

Tyler Mercier
Chris Mercier

ISBN: **1478223383**
ISBN-13: **978-1478223382**

Library of Congress Control Number: **2012-915790**

Photos, art, layout, and design by authors.

CONTENTS

INTRODUCTION

We were inspired to write this book about moving to Hawaii Island after meeting many people who were exasperated with the complexities of relocating to a remote island and disappointed with their life in Hawaii. This book describes our move to Hawaii Island and covers topics that are important to consider before relocating to Hawaii. The frustration of setting up a household on the island can take away the joy of being in Hawaii. This book covers in detail how to set up utilities and services to make the transition to living in Hawaii County easier. It also has resources to help in searching for jobs, neighborhoods, schools, and activities on the island.

We moved to Hawaii to make a dramatic change from our stressful, sedentary life in foggy Northern California to a relaxing, active lifestyle in sunny Hawaii. We lived in Hilo for two wonderful years where we learned about Hawaiian culture, yard care in a rain forest, eating local food, and the importance of house design in the tropics. We moved to Kailua-Kona on the opposite side of the island to experience living in a different climate zone and community. Watching older athletes train on Ali'i Drive in Kona motivated us to get in better shape and cut back our daily calories. We continue to explore communities and climate zones on the island.

Much of the information in this book is available on our website, hiloliving.com, which we created to support newcomers to Hilo. This book is focused on planning and moving logistics and not on whether living in Hawaii is the right choice for you and your family. Though this book is primarily about moving to Hawaii Island, much of the material is applicable to moving to other islands in the state.

Chapter One
A MOVE TO HAWAII ISLAND

Why We Chose the Island of Hawaii

Southern Coast of Hawaii Island

For years we dreamed of moving to Hawaii and our vacations became explorations in finding the best island for us. We have spent time on six of the Hawaiian Islands and love them all, but we found big differences in the cost of living.

Hawaii State has a great diversity in places to live from the remote islands of Lanai and Molokai with

3

small populations to the cosmopolitan city of Honolulu with traffic that competes with any major city in the United States. However, we found the most reasonable costs for rent and food in Hilo, on the eastern side of Hawaii Island.

Hilo town across Hilo Bay

We were charmed by Hilo's tropical climate, farmer's markets, fish shops, astronomy center, parks, and many varied activities. During an extended vacation to the town, we found rentals in Hilo to be substantially less than what we were paying in California.

Our primary focus on lowering our cost of living was rent, because it was our largest monthly expense in California. We found rental houses near the University of Hawaii in Hilo with panoramic views of Hilo Bay for one third the amount we paid for an old, cramped apartment in

Cupertino, California. Rents in Hilo were lower than places we investigated on Oahu and Maui and lower than homes on the western side of Hawaii Island at the time.

Cattle grazing on Hawaii Island

Finding wild fish, grass-fed beef, and fresh produce in Northern California was a constant frustration for us. We were amazed at the availability and bounty of food on Hawaii Island. Every day fishing boats unload their catch of the finest Pacific Ocean fish in Hilo and Kona harbors. Cattle graze on acres of lush grass covering Mauna Kea Volcano. Local grass-fed meats and fresh fish are far less expensive on Hawaii Island than what we paid in California or elsewhere in Hawaii because there are no shipping charges.

Fresh Pacific Tuna (Ahi) from Hilo

Farmer's markets on Hawaii Island sell local grown vegetables, tropical fruits, nuts, seeds, coffees, herbs, mushrooms, and colorful flowers.

Produce from Hilo Farmers Market

Bananas in our backyard in Hilo

We were eager to spend more time in the sunshine, particularly during the dark, cold winters in Northern California. Although it rains most days on the east side of Hawaii Island, the sun shines in Hilo between rain showers. In addition, the tropical climate in Hilo was quite comfortable for us, even without air conditioning.

Hawaii Island is very remote with a small population, but we have found an abundance of intellectually stimulating and interesting cultural activities. Every day we are glad we chose the island as our home and thankful to be living in Hawaii.

Story of our Move to Hilo

Containers arriving by barge to Hilo Harbor

Though we dreamed of living in Hawaii and planned for it incessantly, ironically our move to Hawaii was sudden and "unplanned". At the end of September 2007, we found ourselves suddenly out of a job without prospects for employment. The cost of living in Silicon Valley was astronomical and even with our good income we felt the quality of our life to be very low.

We calculated that we could live several years on our savings in Hilo, Hawaii and live in a superior rental, eat fresher foods, and be in a warmer climate than we could by remaining in Cupertino. The realization that living in Hawaii was an option, and actually made sense in our situation, motivated us to focus all our efforts on planning a move. Our urgency was driven by the promise of reducing our cost of living, lowering our stress, and getting healthy in Hawaii.

Though we had moved across the United States many times, this was the first time that we would be paying for the move ourselves and the first time we were shipping our belongings across an ocean instead of having them loaded onto a truck. We had to minimize the expenses of the move and quickly settle into an affordable rental house in Hilo to keep the cost low. Furthermore, we had limited time to make many decisions about what to bring and how much of the move to do ourselves versus using a moving company.

Initially, we wanted to leave open the possibility of moving back to California after a couple of years, if the right job opened up. It seemed logical to put everything in storage and rent a furnished place in Hawaii. However, when the cost of storing our belongings for three years was added to the extra cost of renting a furnished home in Hawaii, it was cheaper for us to move everything to Hawaii.

Though we had been downsizing our belongings since selling our house the year before, we still had an apartment filled with furniture, books, and electronics as well as a storage area packed with boxes of art, photos, and more books. We had lived in the tropics in high school, so when we selected what to ship, we left behind anything we feared would attract bugs like overstuffed furniture and pine wood bookshelves. We gave away clothes, books, and furniture and brought TVs, game consoles, movies, and books. We also brought folding bookcases, desks, and bedding. We planned to buy new living room furniture in Hawaii.

We estimated that our boxes and furniture would be cheaper to ship in a container than via air freight. Shipping containers come in sizes of 40 feet and 20 feet in length and we hoped our belongings would fit into the smaller size container. We put masking tape on the floor, 7.5 feet wide by 19 feet long, to represent the inside dimensions of a 20 foot container and calculated that the boxes and furniture in our apartment, combined with our boxes in storage, would fit into the space when stacked 7.5 feet high.

Once we settled how to move our belongings, we used an online estimate tool provided by Matson, one of the largest shipping companies to Hawaii, to calculate the shipping cost. Matson's door-to-door service means they drive a container to your site and leave it parked on a chassis for a couple of days, and then return to drive it to the harbor to be loaded on to their ship. The loading and unloading of the container and any storage of the contents were not included in the price.

20 foot Matson container in California

We considered packing and loading the container ourselves to save money, but once we understood the task, we realized it was overwhelming. We had boxes in two locations and our apartment was up a flight of stairs. The container is left parked on a chassis which puts it above shoulder level and it does not come with an elevator or ramp. Furthermore, a wall must be constructed inside the container to keep the boxes from shifting during their travel at sea. Considering the amount of physical labor and our relatively poor physical condition, we were quickly convinced that movers would be worth the cost.

We solicited bids from several local and national moving companies that advertised that they shipped to Hawaii. Armed with prices from Matson, we knew how much the companies were charging for their portion of the move which included packing the apartment, collecting our boxes in storage, loading the container in California, and unloading the container in Hilo. The bids we received were extremely high and their knowledge of shipping to Hawaii was disappointing. We had a lucky break when we contacted a moving company in Hilo that was willing to give us advice about moving from the mainland. Big Isle Moving and Draying, which had great references online, told us they had had good luck working with a company in San Diego, Unipack. We contacted Unipack and everything fell into place. Their prices were reasonable and we were able to specify the container size, shipping company, and use of Big Isle Moving as the receiving company on the Hilo side. They had a crew in Northern California and were amenable to picking up boxes at two locations. They had no problem with scheduling the move to coincide with the next Matson ship to Northern California. We were also able to purchase insurance for our belongings which gave us peace of mind.

Our next decision was whether to bring our cars or buy one in Hawaii. We had two older cars, which we liked a lot and were in good mechanical condition, but seemed inappropriate for Hawaii Island. We envisioned having a four-wheel drive truck instead of two commuter cars. Assuming we would sell our cars in California, we began calling car dealers on Hawaii Island to get prices and availability of used trucks and older SUVs. We were stunned at the high prices they quoted us, easily 3 to 4 times higher than California prices. For comparison we researched what it would cost us to replace the cars we had; one of the cars, an older Ford T-Bird with 70,000 miles valued at about $850 in California, would cost between $3500 and $5000 to replace in Hawaii. It seemed crazy to us to pay $1000 to ship a car "worth" $850. However, it would save us about $2800 to do just that.

We shipped both of our cars and have been glad we did. With acid rain from the volcano, the ocean spray, and the sand and wet towels they have endured, we are happy we did not buy a new car to be abused by island living. We have had use of our cars for five years and plan to keep them for as long as possible. We used Pasha Hawaii Transport Lines and were happy with their service. They picked up the cars in Cupertino for a fee, which saved us the time driving them to their pickup site in Hayward. The cars arrived in Hilo twenty days after the Pasha pickup and they were easy to collect near the harbor in Hilo.

Once we had set the date for the movers and the pickup of the cars, we booked our flight to Hawaii, a rental car, and a local hotel to stay in during our last couple of days in Northern California. We also scheduled hotel rooms in Kona, Volcano, and Hilo to spend the time during our first weeks in

Hawaii. We organized our belongings into piles of what to take with us in luggage, what to ship in the container, and what to leave behind. We thoroughly cleaned the cars since they have to be free from foliage and bugs to get through Hawaii's agriculture control.

We had a tight schedule on the California side of the move because the week of Thanksgiving was approaching so if we missed our flight, we would have to wait three days in California to get past the holiday crush of airline travel. Our cheap tickets to Hawaii were not valid during popular travel times like Thanksgiving.

The first day of our move started at our storage area in San Jose, where the movers met us with a large truck to pick up the boxes we had stored. The movers repacked some of the boxes as they loaded them onto their truck. They followed our car to our apartment in Cupertino where a 20 foot Matson container had just been delivered to the parking lot. The movers were able to back their truck up against the Matson container and carry the boxes from storage into the Matson container. When that was complete, they set up a ramp they had brought to load the boxes and furniture from the apartment.

A half dozen workers rapidly packed the contents of our apartment and carried the boxes and furniture down the stairs and up the ramp into the shipping container.

Loading the Matson container from a moving truck

After packing the boxes and furniture tightly, they built a wooden wall inside the container that was set against the boxes so nothing would shift during the journey. The container was then closed up and a wire seal attached in such a way that the seal would be obviously broken if the container door was opened before it reached its destination. When the Matson container pulled out of the parking lot, we drove to a local hotel and collapsed in exhaustion. We had selected a hotel with a breakfast bar so we would not have to spend time waiting for breakfast in the morning.

Movers loading shipping container in California

The next day, we returned to the apartment in time for Pasha Hawaii Transport Lines to pick up our two cars. A single tow truck was able to carry one of the cars on top and tow the other behind. We cleaned the apartment, disposed of everything left inside, and turned the keys over to the apartment complex manager. The following day we had a quick breakfast at the hotel, loaded up our suitcases, and drove in morning rush hour traffic to the airport in Oakland. We turned in the rental car and boarded our flight to Kona. Once on the airplane we were able to celebrate and relax. Thus far, everything had gone according to plan.

When we arrived in Kona, we rented a car and stayed in a small unit in the Kona Islander Inn on Ali'i Drive over the weekend. We had several weeks before our cars and container would arrive and with the Thanksgiving holiday quickly approaching, we took the time to relax and get on Hawaii time. We spent a few days at the Kailua Lodge in Volcano town to start acclimating to the slower pace in Hawaii. We have enjoyed hiking the paths in Volcanoes National Park in the past, so we were eager to do it again. We finally arrived in Hilo in the late afternoon the day before Thanksgiving and checked into the Hilo Hawaiian Hotel.

Hilo Hawaiian Hotel

Timing our move during the Thanksgiving holiday meant that everything was closed. We checked the classifieds for rentals in the local papers, but there were very few listings and those that we called did not respond to our inquiries. We drove through many of the neighborhoods in Hilo and nearby Puna to get familiar with the area.

We took a journal with us and everywhere we went, we wrote down the time we left, when we arrived, and how many miles it was from the main part of Hilo. We were amazed at the size of the Puna District and the amount of time it took to drive there from Hilo town. Though we saw some wonderful rentals in Puna for low prices, when we added the cost of gas to drive to town, the rents for houses in Hilo looked cheaper.

We originally booked the hotel in Hilo for five nights, but that time quickly passed, so we extended our hotel stay and car rental. We tried to use a local property management company in town, but we found their long application process too frustrating. Being patient and waiting for the right rental house was a challenge. We were still on mainland time our first month on the island and it felt like people were moving in slow motion. We spent our time driving the neighborhoods and trying to relax

A week after arriving in Hilo, an advertisement in the paper caught our eye for a rental house in a neighborhood that we had already decided we liked. We talked to the owner who lived in town and was looking for renters to immediately move into his property. He showed us the house that evening and we loved it. The house was the perfect size and had the view of Hilo Bay that we had dreamt about. We gave him a deposit on the spot to start our 6 month lease for December 1st.

View of Hilo Bay

With a signed lease, we were able to set up most of our utilities in Hilo before moving in. We obtained a box at the post office with the lease and started forwarding our mail. We purchased a couch, bed, and dining table at Furnitureland in Hilo and set up delivery for the following Monday, December 3rd. We set up electric service, water service, sewer service, and internet service.

We were able to determine that our container had arrived on the island from Matson's website and we called the local moving company to set up delivery of the container to our Hilo address. After 11 days in the hotel, we checked out, bought airbeds at Wal-Mart, and moved into our rental home in Hilo. Though our new furniture was delivered, there was no sign of our Matson container and the moving company was unable to give us a delivery date. We eventually found out that our container had been delivered to Kawaihae harbor on the west side of the island instead of Hilo harbor where we assumed it would arrive. Delivery of our container was delayed several days because the moving company had to drive to the other side of the island to fetch it in Kawaihae. When the moving company finally drove the container to our house and unloaded it, we were delighted to find that nothing was missing or broken.

We found an auto insurance company for our cars in advance of their arrival in Hilo. Pasha emailed us that their ship carrying our cars was due into Hilo harbor, so we set up a pickup time. We went to Harpers near Hilo Harbor where Pasha leaves the vehicles and obtained a signed bill of lading needed to get Hawaii titles for the cars. We were happy to be driving our own cars again and to drop off the rental car at Hilo airport. We spent the next couple of days finalizing our car insurance and getting safety inspections, Hawaii car titles, and license plates for the cars.

After five weeks, our move to Hawaii was complete and it was a wonderful feeling to be settled in and reunited with all our belongings.

Chapter Two
WHERE TO LIVE ON HAWAII ISLAND

Choosing a Location on the Island

Hapuna Beach on Hawaii Island

In Hawaii, locations that are short distances apart can have dramatic variations in climate and cultural diversity. The differences within sixty miles on Hawaii Island can be greater in weather and lifestyle than the differences between Phoenix, Arizona and Portland, Oregon. Thinking of Hawaii as an entire "continent" has helped us to clarify the vast number of choices we have in climate, culture, job opportunities, and cost of living when selecting a location to live. In addition to considering the cost of rent when we chose our home on Hawaii Island, we evaluated the amount of rainfall, temperature, remoteness, risk of flooding, and volcanic activity in different communities and neighborhoods.

Climate: The island of Hawaii has the climatic diversity of a large continent. The many climate zones are due to the heights of Mauna Kea and Mauna Loa Volcanoes, the trade winds, and local wind circulation that creates many micro-climates.

Arctic zone - The summits of Mauna Kea and Mauna Loa Volcanoes, at 13,796 and 13,333 feet respectively, to 9800 feet above sea level have Arctic climates where the soil is permanently frozen.

Temperate zones - Over two thirds of Hawaii Island is in one of three temperate climate zones at altitudes from 1600 to 9800 feet above sea level. The largest temperate zone, from 1600 to 6500 feet, has warm temperatures and year round rainfall. The towns of Volcano and Waimea are located in this climate zone.

Desert zones – A hot, arid zone on the northwestern coast of Hawaii Island is created by the volcanoes blocking the rain clouds. The desert along the Kohala Coast has the driest weather in the state of Hawaii with less than ten inches of rain a year. The biggest resorts on Hawaii Island are located there to guarantee visitors a sunny and warm vacation.

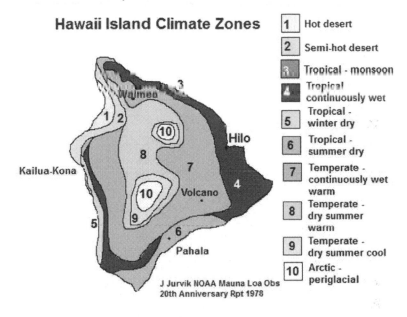

Hawaii Island Climate Zones

1	Hot desert
2	Semi-hot desert
3	Tropical - monsoon
4	Tropical continuously wet
5	Tropical - winter dry
6	Tropical - summer dry
7	Temperate - continuously wet warm
8	Temperate - dry summer warm
9	Temperate - dry summer cool
10	Arctic - periglacial

J Jurvik NOAA Mauna Loa Obs
20th Anniversary Rpt 1978

<u>Tropical zones</u> - The most populated areas of the island, from sea level to 1600 feet, are in one of the four tropical climate zones with the greatest amount of annual rainfall. The rainfall varies considerably, from 60 to 300 inches a year, depending on a specific area's elevation and whether it is facing the trade winds or protected from them.

When you select a community on the island, find out how much annual rainfall it gets. Differences can be dramatic even within a town, where one neighborhood may get hundreds more inches of rain than a neighborhood higher up the mountain or closer to the coast.

Tsunami signs posted around Hawaii Island

Flooding: Tsunamis are a real threat in Hawaii. Since moving to Hawaii, we have had three tsunami evacuations. In Hilo we lived above the tsunami evacuation zone, but during a tsunami alert our landlord moved his merchandise into our garage because his business was located in the tsunami flood zone in town. In Kona, we were evacuated twice during tsunami alerts, the second time after the 2011 earthquake in Japan. That tsunami damaged streets, houses, and structures in Kona when ocean water rushed into Kailua Bay. Living above a tsunami evacuation zone avoids you having to spend the night in your car at a higher elevation during a tsunami alert.

Properties in flood zones and along the coast can be inundated with water during heavy rains and high tides. Homes in flood zones tend to have more problems with mold, mildew, and bugs.

Hawaii Island's very active Kilauea Volcano

Volcanoes: The currently active Volcano and potential for four other Volcanoes to become active are ever present on Hawaii Island. Lava and volcanic emissions, called Vog (volcanic smog), are produced by Kilauea Volcano and earthquakes affect the entire island.

The Vog settles around the island depending upon the winds, but the Ka'u and Kona Districts on the southwestern side of the island usually get the most. In Kona, the Vog moves up the mountain as the day heats up, so the differences in air quality can be substantial even with small increases in elevation. Air quality and earthquake

25

preparedness are things to consider when selecting a location to live on the island.

Remote home on a lava field on Hawaii Island

Remoteness: Hawaii Island has many remote residential areas that appeal to those looking for low cost rentals and low real estate prices. Many remote areas have no county services like water, sewer, and road maintenance. Internet and phone access may also be limited. Some areas are completely off-the-grid and use solar energy or gas-powered generators for electricity. Residents rely on rain water collected in tanks and must haul in their drinking water. Crime is a problem, particularly theft, in many remote locations. Police and fire protection is limited making insurance difficult to obtain for vehicles and belongings. A long driving distance to shopping can become a financial burden with the high cost of gasoline in Hawaii.

Finding Your Neighborhood

Hawaii style houses

Once you have selected an area on the island based on climate, proximity to a job, or other factors, there is still the neighborhood to choose. Neighborhoods vary greatly and living in one that does not suit your lifestyle can be miserable.

Noise is a bigger problem than most places on the mainland. Houses and condominiums are close together and windows and doors are always open in Hawaii to catch the breezes. Walls are usually thin in homes since insulation is not needed in the tropics. Sounds and smells from neighbors, nearby roads, and parks are hard to ignore.

The biggest noise annoyances are from dogs, cars, coqui frogs, and loud parties. Just because a neighborhood is quiet during the day does not mean that coqui frogs and screeching of tires (drifting is a popular night time sport in Hawaii) are not a problem at night.

Hawaii Island condominium in Kona

The neighborhoods in Hilo vary considerably, some filled with students attending the University of Hawaii, some with mostly retirees, and others with younger families. When we were looking for a neighborhood in Hilo, we drove around the hills above Hilo Bay and surveyed the homes and views. Some neighborhoods had homes with broken down cars and trash in their front yards while others had houses surrounded with flower beds and Japanese gardens.

Though we were focused on Hilo, we also scoped out Puna and its many residential areas. Puna is one of the fastest growing areas in the state. New businesses and services are opening and adding to its appeal. Though the rents were lower, we ruled out the Puna area because of the long drive into Hilo.

Hilo University Heights area with Mauna Kea overhead

We wanted to be close to Hilo shopping, above the tsunami evacuation zone, in a quiet neighborhood with a view of Hilo Bay. Having selected the area above Hilo town near the post office, farmer's market, and mall, we focused our search on a small number of neighborhoods. When a rental became available on one of the streets we had identified, we immediately jumped on the opportunity.

Renting in Hawaii

There are numerous types of rentals in Hawaii, which is a benefit and a challenge when looking for a home on the island. The tourist industry has created a large number of time-shares and vacation rentals catering to visitors. Long-term apartments, condominiums, and houses are also available.

Kona ocean view condominiums

Vacation rentals are advertised in the newspapers and on websites. These rentals are reserved with credit cards and usually have pictures of every room, details about the property, and reviews by people who have stayed there. These rentals usually come with amenities like ocean views, swimming pools, and other benefits in a condominium complex or gated community. They are usually furnished and advertise daily, weekly, and monthly rental prices. Rental prices change over the year and can be widely variable depending on how well tourism is doing that year.

Apartments in Hilo

Many long term rentals in Hawaii are available through property management companies. The reason for this is that Hawaii law requires all rentals to have a Hawaii resident as a legal contact for the property. In many cases, owners who rent their house or condominium use a local real estate or property management company as their representative in Hawaii. These agents advertise the rentals, show the place, pay the Hawaii general excise tax, repair the property, and are part of the lease negotiation.

Golf course condominiums on Hawaii Island

Most property managers require that you fill out an application form and pay for processing the application. The application requires personal references, job history, bank account numbers, and addresses where you have lived for the past 5 to 10 years. Then you wait. While they are "processing" the application, they will not show or discuss available properties even to let you decide if you are interested in renting them.

Property managers advertise their rentals in newspapers and on web pages, usually without addresses and minimal pictures. We applied with a property management company that advertised in the local Hilo newspaper, hoping they could help us with our house rental search. Their application process consisted of a credit check and contacting our references, banks, and previous landlords.

Beach front living on Hawaii Island

After a week of waiting, we went to the property management office and demanded our paperwork back. We were dismayed to see our application with bank account and social security numbers on a desk in plain view of workers and visitors in the office.

For us, the best option for renting in Hawaii has been to deal directly with the owners. Owners are usually more selective about their renters, keep the property in good condition, and know everything about the place. We have learned the value of a good landlord and being able to get in touch with them to resolve issues.

Hawaii has problems with rental scams which usually involve an "amazing" deal on a great property where all you have to do is send payment in advance to secure it. When you arrive the place may not exist, or be a foreclosed property, or have no water and electricity available. Be wary of any deal that looks too good.

We have heard of some lucky folks getting help from realtors in advance of their arrival. Some have even signed a lease sight unseen. In Hawaii, with the "diversity" of neighborhoods and the unknowns about the condition of a house or apartment, we would not recommend signing a lease for a rental that you have not personally inspected. You do not want to find out that the home you signed a year lease for is infested with cockroaches or filled with mold.

If you decide to take the property management route to find a rental, it is best to submit your application before you arrive to save yourself the expense of staying in a hotel while the staff calls your references.

Finding Your Ideal Hawaii Home

Luxury House on Hawaii Island

Living in a house designed for the tropical climate of Hawaii is so important we wrote a book on the subject, *Your Ideal Hawaii Home: Avoid Disaster when Buying or Building in Hawaii.* We recommend renting on the island before buying or building to make sure the climate and neighborhood are what you expected.

We have noticed that people from the mainland are attracted to houses in Hawaii that are similar to the style of houses where they just came from, even if the design is completely unsuited to Hawaii's tropical climate. After experiencing the weather, humidity, insects, yard work, and neighborhood you may change your opinion of the type and location of the home you want in Hawaii.

There are many design considerations when selecting a home in Hawaii. An apartment, condominium, or house in Hawaii should have excellent airflow to keep it cool, reduce the humidity, and minimize the electric bill. Windows should be able to open and be positioned to allow air to flow through the home. Windows should be shaded from the sun by low-overhanging eaves and protected so that they can stay open even when it is pouring rain outside. Fans are cheaper to run than air conditioning and a necessity to keep cool when the breezes stop.

A hip-roof is best for rain and high winds

Hawaii's tropical climate causes rapid growth of lawns, flowers, trees, and fruit. Mowing, trimming, weeding, bug control, and hauling green waste to the dump can be exhausting in Hawaii's hot, humid climate. Lack of yard

36

maintenance can quickly cause problems like attracting loud coqui frogs, crawling bugs, and plugging drainage ditches.

Tropical growth overtakes a home in East Hawaii

We were surprised at the overwhelming amount of work required to maintain the small yard of our Hilo rental. The high monthly cost of gasoline to mow our lawn two to three times a week, herbicide to control weeds under the house, and pesticide to keep the ants and termites under control was unexpected. During the year, there was never a break in the sprouting of new palm leaves, crops of lemons and bananas, and rapid growth of the grass.

Some rental houses come with yard care, which can be a big savings of time and expense. Living in a condominium or apartment may be a good choice for those who want to avoid gardening in the tropics altogether.

Gated community on Hawaii Island

Chapter Three
PLANNING AND MOVE LOGISTICS

Timing your Move to Hawaii

Arriving at Kona airport

If we could have picked the time of year that we moved to Hawaii, we would have moved sometime between April 1st and September 30th. Hawaii is a popular destination during the winter months which makes prices higher and the rental market tighter. Visitors and short-term residents start to leave in the spring so more rentals and homes become available and prices for airfare, hotels, rent, and food tend to be lower.

We moved to Hawaii Island at the worst time, a month before Christmas when the island was filled with tourists and part-time residents. The timing worked out extremely well for us, so we have come to feel that the best time to move to Hawaii is any time you can make it happen.

A move to Hawaii requires a place to stay while finding a long term rental or home to purchase. We stayed in a hotel for two weeks while looking for a rental in Hilo. If we had it to do again, we would have stayed in a vacation rental with a kitchen instead of a cramped hotel room.

When budgeting for your move to Hawaii, prepare for delays in receiving your car and belongings. Bad weather, a strike or any number of other things can slow down delivery. Having flexibility in your schedule and money to absorb a delay will help make the move smoother and less stressful.

What to Bring to Hawaii

We have met people who arrived in Hawaii with two suitcases and furnished their new house in several months from garage sales. Some people sell everything before coming, while others stash their belongings in a storage unit on the mainland or leave them in another house they still own. What you choose to bring with you or leave behind will make a difference in the cost of your move as well as your cost of living once you are in Hawaii.

Some people put their possessions in a storage unit on the mainland to save on the cost of moving to Hawaii. Assuming a monthly storage cost of $250 to $350, in two years the overall storage cost will be close to the $7000 it would have cost to move them. Those costs do not include the expense of flying back to the mainland to visit, later transport, or dispose of the things left behind. Similarly, maintaining another house full of possessions remotely can be expensive over many years. If your plan is to live full-time in Hawaii for many years, then the long term cost of storing your belongings should be compared to the cost of moving them as well as not being able to use and enjoy them.

Some people hope to keep their moving costs lower by planning to buy everything in Hawaii after they arrive. In our experience, prices for new furniture, kitchenware, bedding, etc. are at least 30% more than on the mainland and on Hawaii Island there is limited selection. Hawaii has many furnished rentals which offer the option of moving without bringing any furniture or kitchenware. However, having your own furnishings can save on the cost of a long term rental, as furnished homes tend to cost 20 to 40% more.

The downside of bringing all of your possessions to Hawaii is that island homes tend to be smaller than mainland homes. One family we met brought two 40 foot containers of furnishings for their new home in Hawaii. Years later, they still have a shipping container parked next to their house filled with their excess belongings.

We started "downsizing" our possessions years before we moved to Hawaii by having garage sales, giving car loads of stuff to Goodwill, and hiring people to haul away things that were too heavy for us to move. We were surprised at how much we had packed into a 2200 square foot house in 10 years. We estimate we reduced our belongings by more than 70% over two years, but even so we filled a 20 foot shipping container when we moved to Hawaii.

Since moving to Hawaii, we have had time to read the books we have been collecting for years and enjoy the movies and music we brought. We have had time to sort through boxes of photographs and every year we put up the fake Christmas tree we brought and reminisce while hanging our collection of tree ornaments.

We still have stacks of boxes that have not been opened in Hawaii with things that are precious to us. Initially, we stored our unpacked boxes in the garage of our rental house in Hilo, however, when we moved to a smaller condominium in Kona without a garage we had to rent a storage unit.

During visits to our storage unit in Kona over the past few years, we have watched the continuing drama of an elderly couple and their 50-something year old children with a storage unit near ours. During the family's visitations to their storage unit, the elderly couple sits in chairs facing the open unit stacked to the ceiling with boxes as their children carefully unpack one box at a time. We have watched them unpack gleaming ceramics from the Orient, which from afar look like museum pieces. As each piece is held, the couple recounts the story of a trip or adventure when it was acquired. Their children interrupt to try and convince them to sell it. A few treasures are taken away, but most items are carefully repacked and returned to the stack of boxes.

After watching this family's drama over the years, we look at our own stack of boxes that we cannot seem to part with and realize how many treasured memories they represent for us. Everyone we know has similar collections of treasures that they brought with them to Hawaii or left behind on the mainland. We are glad to have our treasures with us in Hawaii so we can enjoy them, but we also realize that there is a cost in time, money, and mobility for us to hold on to them.

Reducing our stuff at a garage sale in Kona

Shipping or Buying Cars in Hawaii

If you ship your car to Hawaii, companies like Pasha Hawaii Transport Lines and Matson Navigation will transport them from the West Coast of the United States to most of the islands in Hawaii. You can ship vehicles in a container if you prefer to not have them driven onto the ship.

Car dealership in Hilo Hawaii

A car transported to the island should be in good working condition to withstand the tropical heat, salty air, and rough roads on Hawaii Island, particularly if you plan to live in a remote area. There may not be a dealer on the island that does manufacturer's certified repairs for your type of car. Furthermore, it may be substantially more expensive to do repairs or maintenance on your car in Hawaii than on the mainland. Good mechanics are in high demand and even minor repairs are usually expensive and take a long time since parts are rarely kept in stock.

If you plan to buy a new car after moving to Hawaii Island, be aware that new cars typically sell for list price plus additional costs, like shipping, undercoating, and other dealer add-ons. If you are used to shopping for a new car armed with a dealers invoice price report to get the best price, you may just get a laugh from the sales people in Hawaii when you attempt to negotiate. Most car dealerships on the island have a small inventory of new cars and they are aware that their nearest competition is a long way away. A lengthy price negotiation is undesirable if you are paying $350 a week for a rental car.

Car dealers know it takes six weeks or more for a car to be shipped to the island after purchasing it online or from a dealer on the mainland. Shipping costs will run at least $1000 and there may be additional costs to get the car to the shipping dock on the mainland side and picked up on the Hawaii side. Once the car is in Hawaii it must be registered with the state and the tax, title, and license fees paid. It is even more expensive to fly back to the mainland to buy a vehicle. The time and cost to buy a new car remotely helps to explain why car dealers on the island feel they can get full price or more for their new cars.

If you plan to buy a used car after moving, you may find limited selection and high prices on the island. A used car priced at $800 on the mainland may sell for $3,000 to $5,000 on Hawaii Island and most cars sell for more than blue book prices. Used cars may have damage from driving on lava roads, mold, and rust.

Used car lot in Kona

We moved our two older cars to Hawaii and assumed that we would replace them in a year or two. Fortunately, both cars are still running after five years on rough roads with volcanic emissions, sea spray, and many beach trips. Since we have been able to get repairs and keep them in working order, we are happy we brought them.

When we need to replace a car, we plan to take the advice of local mechanics and buy a used car on Oahu. Oahu has over 2/3 of the cars in the state and is a small island with better paved roads. Used cars usually have lower mileage and less wear and tear. Oahu has a large military population who need to sell their cars quickly when they are ordered to move, which makes deals on used cars available.

Transporting your Possessions to Hawaii

Matson ship arriving in Hilo with shipping containers

If everything you plan to move fits into a stack of boxes, then US mail or air freight may be the cheapest and easiest way to transport them. However, if you are bringing furniture and stacks of boxes, it may be cheaper to transport them in a shipping container.

When you mail or air freight boxes, you need an address and person to receive them in Hawaii. We have spoken to several new self-storage businesses on Hawaii Island that are happy to accept your boxes sent through US mail, Federal Express, United Parcel Service or other air freight companies for a fee.

If you move your belongings in a shipping container, you can set up everything yourself with the shipping company directly or have a moving company handle the loading and transportation of the container to Hawaii.

Matson Navigation Company and Horizon Lines have the largest fleets from the West Coast of the United States to Hawaii. Pasha Hawaii Transport Lines, which specializes in shipping vehicles to Hawaii, also transports containers. Matson is a Hawaii based company and we found their website to have the most information and best tools to estimate the cost of shipping a container.

Even if you leave the transportation logistics to a moving company, knowing the cost to ship a container from the mainland to Hawaii helps you to evaluate bids from moving companies. Standard shipping container sizes are 20 foot and 40 foot in length. According to Matson, the furnishings of a three bedroom home will fill a 20-foot container.

We knew our belongings would fit into a 20 foot container because we had marked out the inside dimensions of the container in our living room to verify that the space was adequate. Our preference was to have our own container because that way the seal would not be broken until the container was delivered to us in Hawaii. We told the moving company that we wanted to use Matson when we requested a bid because their shipping schedule matched our travel plans.

The moving company brought a Matson container to our apartment parking lot in California to load it. We watched as they loaded it and wrote down the container number to track its trip to Hawaii on Matson's website.

Some moving companies consolidate freight from several owners into one shipping container to save on transportation costs.

Freight packed to share a shipping container

If you decide to load a shipping container yourself, rather than use a moving company, the shipping company will deliver and pick up the container at your location. The shipping companies do not provide ramps, lift-gates, tie-downs, or materials for packing or loading. The containers are left on a chassis which brings it to shoulder level or higher. Loading a container takes expertise to pack it so that the contents remain secured during an ocean voyage. Once the container is loaded, a wooden wall is usually constructed inside to help keep the contents from shifting.

Shipping container delivered on a chassis

When selecting the best way for you to transport your belongings to Hawaii, the cost, complexity, and amount of time in transition are considerations. Other things like getting your belongings insured, the cost of storage on either side of the trip, and the proximity of the shipping port on the mainland need to be evaluated.

Movers packing a container using a ramp and flatbed truck

Bringing Pets to Hawaii

Hawaii Kitty Cat

Moving your pets to Hawaii takes a lot of advanced planning. Hawaii is rabies-free partly because of the special rules about bringing animals to the islands. Hawaii law, which is administered by the Hawaii Department of Agriculture, applies to all dogs, cats, service animals, kittens, and puppies. The law requires that animals be put in quarantine for up to 120 days, but there is a provision for direct release and a "5-day-or-less-program" if certain steps are taken in advance.

To qualify for the state's direct release program, your pets must have received at least two rabies vaccines 30 days or more apart that have been verified by a successful blood test and wait 120 days before arriving in Hawaii. The pet must also have a working electronic microchip implanted. If you research the specific requirements and get the paper work needed in advance, your pet may qualify to be immediately released to you at the Honolulu or Kona airport. The laws, rules, and procedures can change, so verify everything before your move.

There are some breeds of non-domestic cats and dogs that are prohibited in Hawaii such as wolf, dingo, Bengal, and others. And there are rules for bringing in other types of pets such as birds, fish, turtles, horses, and livestock. There are also rules about importing plants, microorganisms, and non-domestic animals to Hawaii.

All dogs four months or older must be licensed by state law and must have their license on their collars at all times. Once on Hawaii Island, you need to register your dog at one of the Hawaii Island Humane Society locations in Kona, Keaau, or Waimea. Shelters are closed on Sunday and holidays. The owner of a dog must be 18 or older and must provide their name, address, microchip number, and contact information. Owners must also provide their dog's name, breed, age, sex, and a veterinarian certificate if the dog is spayed or neutered. For a service dog, the appropriate documentation must be submitted with the application.

Big Island Humane Society in Kona

Hawaii is not a pet-friendly place for renters. It is hard to find a house, condominium, or apartment willing to rent to someone with a pet. Many housing and condominium complexes have no-dog or no-pet rules.

At the same time barking dogs, feral cats, and roosters are a problem on the island and can keep you up night after night. The Hawaii Island Humane Society is actively working to protect animals from cruelty, provide problem solving techniques for neighbors dealing with noisy dogs and animals, and is a great resource for pet owners in Hawaii.

Bringing Guns to Hawaii

Unlike many other states in the United States, the use of deadly force for protection of personal property is not justifiable in Hawaii and it is not considered defensive if you initiate the use of deadly force with a gun. Police will make an arrest in any homicide regardless of the justifiable use of a firearm and sort out whether to bring charges later. In addition, you are not protected against a civil suit by a home intruder if you use force against them if they were only there to commit theft (Civil Liability Act 97). In Hawaii, where theft is the most common crime, you cannot hurt someone for stealing your belongings.

Guns in Hawaii

All firearms brought into Hawaii must be registered within 72 hours at the county police station. Machine guns and "assault pistols" are not permitted in the state. Hawaii prohibits greater than 10 round detachable pistol magazines and even having an empty one is illegal. Stun guns, cannons, silencers, hand grenades, explosives, and bombs are illegal. The state also outlaws Teflon coated ammunition, explosive or segmented ammunition, handguns made of zinc, shotguns with barrels less than 18 inches, and rifles with barrels less than 16 inches. Concealed carry and openly carrying a firearm in public are felonies in Hawaii without a permit from the county chief of police. Generally a permit is only issued to law enforcement, military, and security guards and not to private citizens. The owner of a firearm is liable for personal injury or property damage caused by the discharge of their firearm.

When not in use, guns must be kept unloaded and locked up. When being transported they must be unloaded in rigid lockable receptacles or in a commercial gun container that completely encloses the firearm.

You must show evidence of safety training to get a permit for a handgun. A 6-hour course, including 2 hours on a shooting range and instruction on Hawaii gun laws, safe handling, and storage of a gun, is taught by National Rifle Association (NRA) certified instructors on the island.

If you plan to move guns in your shipping container or luggage, verify Hawaii gun laws in advance as well as Transportation Security Administration (TSA) and individual airline guidelines and rules.

Banking in Hawaii

The big mainland banks like Wells Fargo and Bank of America have no presence in Hawaii. Some people do their banking online and get cash via ATM's from their mainland banks. We closed all our accounts on the mainland and opened accounts in local Hawaii banks which has worked well for us.

Bank of Hawaii

Hawaii has many small banks, though some are subsidiaries of larger companies. The local banks differ in their charges and services so it is worth shopping around to find the best deal. Here are some banking options:

- First Hawaiian Bank was founded in 1858 and is the oldest and largest bank in Hawaii. It is a subsidiary of Banc West Corporation. Banc West is a subsidiary of BNP Paribas, a large European bank.

- Bank of Hawaii Corporation is a regional bank focused on Hawaii, American Samoa, and the Pacific Islands. The company is listed on the New York Stock Exchange as "BOH".

- Hawaii National Bank is a community bank founded in 1960 in Oahu's China town.

- American Savings Bank is Hawaii's third-largest bank founded in 1925. ASB is a subsidiary of Hawaiian Electric Industries (HEI), which also owns Hawaii Island's electric company, HELCO.

- Central Pacific Bank was established in 1954 to serve the needs of small businesses in Hawaii. The company is traded on the New York Stock Exchange under the symbol "CPF".

- HomeStreet Bank is a family and employee-owned private bank serving the Northwest and Hawaii since 1921.

- Territorial Savings Bank is a local bank based in Honolulu and has been providing service in Hawaii since 1921.

Hawaii Federal Credit Union

Hawaii Island has regional credit unions including Independent Employers Group (IEG) Federal Credit Union, Big Island Federal Credit Union, CU Hawaii Federal Credit Union, Hawaii County Employees Federal Credit Union, and HFS Federal Credit Union.

Hawaii American Savings Bank

Bank and credit union ATM's are located in hotels, malls, and grocery stores around the island.

Schools on Hawaii Island

Hawaii's public schools are managed by the State Department of Education (DOE) and members of the State Board of Education are appointed by the Governor of Hawaii. The centralization of the state's schools makes the Department of Education and its budget of $2.5 billion an emotionally charged issue in Hawaii politics. Hawaii's Department of Education and its powerful teacher's union have been criticized for the high dropout rate and low standing on national standardized tests of students in Hawaii's public schools.

Hilo High School

On Hawaii Island, elementary and middle schools within a "school complex" feed a single high school. The ten public high schools and their feeder elementary, middle, and charter schools on the island are administered in three "complex areas".

The Honokaa-Kealakehe-Kohala-Konawaena complex area consists of four high schools, an adult community school, six charter schools, and 14 feeder elementary and middle schools serving the western side of the island. The Hilo-Laupahoehoe-Waiakea complex area consists of three high schools, an adult community school, three charter schools, and 11 feeder elementary and middle schools serving Hilo and the Hamakua Coast. The Kau-Keaau-Pahoa complex area consists of three high schools, five charter schools, and six elementary and middle schools.

Elementary School in Hilo

In addition to the public schools, there are seventeen private schools on the island that provide Waldorf, Montessori, and religious educations as well as private high schools with expensive tuitions that prepare students for college.

We home schooled our son, so we do not have direct experience with the public or private schools in Hawaii. We have heard positive and negative stories from parents about the public schools. Though there are issues with the level of scholastics and problems with violence in some schools, the students we have met attending Hawaii public schools are more happy and less stressed out then students we knew in Northern California.

Hawaii Preparatory Academy in Waimea

When we moved to Hilo it was a stark difference for us to see students pouring out of Hilo High School at the end of the day with open, happy faces compared to public high schools in Silicon Valley where the students emerged with furrowed faces often hidden under hoodies.

In Kona, we lived in a condominium complex with school-age children who had recently arrived in Hawaii. Our observation was that Asian-American children were immediately accepted by their classmates and delighted by their experience of fitting in. Caucasian students had varying experiences in the Hawaii public schools from feeling accepted to being bullied.

St. Joseph's Catholic High School in Hilo

Before deciding to enroll your child in a particular school, we recommend that you visit the school, observe recess, and if possible attend some classes. Though a nearby elementary school may look great, if you plan to stay in Hawaii for many years, find out which middle school and high school the elementary school feeds. On the western side of the island, neighborhoods with local elementary schools are often a very long bus ride to the high school.

Hawaii is supportive of home school families, but the requirements are different than other states. There are groups around Hawaii Island that support home school families and have classes and events for the children.

Waiakea High School Hilo

We have experience with the Hilo Community Adult School which offers GED testing and evening classes. The staff was very helpful in supporting our son passing the GED. Hawaii State also offers a Competency-Based High School Diploma Program which combines taking adult classes and passing the GED to receive a Hawaii High School diploma.

The University of Hawaii at Hilo offers numerous Bachelor's, Master's, and Doctoral degrees and has certification and licensure programs. The University has specialized colleges in agriculture, Hawaiian studies, pharmacy, and astronomy. Community colleges in Hilo and Kona offer Associate Arts degrees and certifications in specializations like auto mechanics, welding, carpentry, hospitality, and the culinary arts.

University of Hawaii Hilo

Japanese culture, from immigrants who started arriving on the island in the early 1900's and residents from Japan, is one of the influences in Hawaii. Like many Asian countries, the Japanese highly regard education and teachers. Academically accomplished students are treated like great athletes are on the mainland. When our son was studying for his GED examination our Japanese friends prayed for his success and even gave him a good luck amulet, an Omamori, to support him passing the test.

When we attended community events and public hearings at Hilo High School, we were surprised at how old and dilapidated everything was in the building. The chairs and the tables looked like they were from the 1960s. Though the metal roof has recently been replaced, at the time it looked like it was about to rust through. Those aging buildings have not kept Hilo High graduates from being accepted to prestigious universities on the mainland. We know of three students within two years who received full scholarships to Harvard and others who were accepted to Stanford and ivy league schools. It may be the food or the sun in Hawaii or perhaps the influence of Asian cultures that value education, but in Hilo and many other towns on Hawaii Island top high school students are highly accomplished.

Library at University of Hawaii at Hilo

Preparing a Budget for Living in Hawaii

We created a budget before moving to Hawaii Island based on our research during previous visits. We had gone to stores and checked online and newspaper advertisements to get an idea of the cost of rent, food, and gasoline. But most of our budget was speculation based on our optimistic estimates of health care costs, insurance, utilities, and food. A budget is a great planning tool, but following it is another matter.

For us, just moving to Hilo immediately reduced our monthly expenses as compared to Northern California. We rented a 3 bedroom house with a garage and a view of Hilo Bay for less than one third of the rent we were paying for an older (1960's) upstairs apartment in Cupertino with half the space and wedged between two noisy freeways. Our food costs also decreased because so many of the foods that we love are less expensive on Hawaii Island than in California, in particular avocados, tomatoes, lettuce, onions, cucumbers, bananas, wild fish, and grass-fed beef.

Below is a list of expenses to consider when planning your budget for living on Hawaii Island:

Rent /Mortgage (plus tax & maintenance fees)
Renters/Home owners Insurance
Electric (HELCO)

Cable and Internet (Oceanic Time Warner)
Water (if there is county service)
Sewer (if there is county service)
Garbage service
Phone and/or Cell phone service
Garden costs (pesticide, herbicide, gas for mowing)
Security (monthly alarm service, video surveillance)
Medical insurance
Storage unit (if required)
PO box rent and/or Bank safe deposit box
Car payment
Car insurance
Car tax & safety sticker (annual fees)
Gasoline ($5/gallon)
Car repairs
School and activities cost
Local foods (fruit, vegetables, fish, local meats)
COSTCO fee (annual)
Mainland products (grains, oils, paper and plastic products, pre-package foods, medicine, supplements, etc.)

Before moving, we calculated how long our savings would last in Hawaii based on the budget we put together. Every expense that we could reduce translated to living in Hawaii longer.

Over the past five years in Hawaii, we have focused on finding ways to further reduce our monthly expenses to make our savings last longer and increase the value of our small income. We track the amount of money we spend each month and constantly look for ways to save money by cutting back on things we do not need. We are always aiming for a higher quality of life for less cost.

Chapter Four
AFTER MOVING TO HAWAII ISLAND

Setting up Utilities and Services

Hawaii County Water Supply Administration Office

Once you have moved to Hawaii Island, you can start to set up your utilities like electricity, water, sewer, telephone, and cable TV as well as services like internet, security, and garbage pickup. You need a signed lease for a rental or closing papers for a house to turn on the water and electricity. You also need a proof of address to rent a box at the US post office or get a Hawaii State identification card.

In most cases setting up electricity, cable, water, and sewer service on Hawaii Island requires that you go to an office in person and wait in a line. We found everyone to be nice and helpful, but it helps to be in *aloha* time rather than in a mainland hurry. No one is thrilled about obnoxious people from the mainland moving to town and if you are in a line to set up utilities everyone knows that you are not a tourist. The best approach is to be very patient.

Some other tips for minimizing the stress of setting up utilities is to go to the county and utility offices as early in the day as possible since there is usually a shorter line and everyone is in a good mood then. Do not try and do everything in one day. We have chuckled at people who flew into town, bought a house, and attempted to get all their utilities set up on a tight schedule before their flight back to the mainland. Their stress and frustration seems to defeat the whole point of them moving to Hawaii.

Sewer Services:
Hawaii County has limited sewer services to waste water treatment facilities in Honokaa, Kealakehe near Kona, Kapehu Camp near Laupahoehoe, Papaikou and Pepeekeo north of Hilo. The Hilo area has one waste water treatment plant which connects to sewer lines available to only a portion of the town. Maps of the county sewer lines are available on Hawaii County's website.

Many houses, condominiums, and buildings on Hawaii Island are not connected to a county sewer system and instead have a septic system or a private sewer system shared by many houses or an entire complex. Private shared sewer systems usually are paid as a part of a monthly homeowner maintenance fee. Unfortunately, Hawaii County has the largest number of cesspools that are out of compliance with Federal EPA standards in the state.

If your home is connected to a county sewer system, you need to set up your water service with Hawaii County first, in order to get the sewer service set up. Once your water service is set up you can go to the County Department of Environmental Management offices (which includes the Wastewater Division) in Hilo or Kona with the account number given to you by the Hawaii County water service and fill out the paperwork.

When we moved to Hilo, we tried to set up the sewer service first and one of the employees there had to explain the process to us. By the time we had set up the water service, it was too late to go back to get the sewer service set up. When we returned to set up the sewer service, the person we had spoken to the day before waved to us as we entered. She remembered our name and told us she had already set everything up for us. We were surprised and very pleased.

Water Services:

County water services are not available to every house or community on Hawaii Island. Some communities have their own water companies and many condominium communities include water service as part of the homeowner's monthly maintenance fee. The limited service area of Hawaii County's water system means that many homes on the island depend on rainfall for their water. Water catchment systems are used to collect rain and must be maintained to minimize rust and keep out bugs and rodents.

Since the 1990's, drought conditions on Hawaii Island and acid rain created by sulfuric gases from the volcano have lowered the quality of water collected from rainfall and made it unsafe to drink. Residents with catchment systems get their drinking water from community water taps.

If your home is connected to a county water service, you must visit the County Department of Water Supply in Hilo, Waimea, Kona, or Ka'u to set up the service. You must show proof of a lease or home purchase, photo identification, and pay a deposit. If the home is also connected to a county sewer service, the county water personnel will provide an account service number to set up your Hawaii County sewer service.

County water bills arrive every other month. Water bills have energy charges detailed which the county adjusts monthly, based on any increases in their cost of electricity.

The cost of pumping water is high in Hawaii and the County Department of Water Supply is the largest customer of the local electric company (HELCO). A third of the water department's budget goes to pay for the energy costs to pump water around the island.

Electric Service:
On Hawaii Island, Hawaii Electric Light Company (HELCO) is the only electric company. The company is a subsidiary of Hawaiian Electric Industries (HEI), which has subsidiaries throughout the state of Hawaii.

HELCO Office in Kona

You can call the electric company to start your service or visit their office in Hilo, Kona, or Waimea. If you need to visit their office, take documentation of your lease or property ownership, photo identification, and be ready to pay a deposit. HELCO has recently installed a website portal to allow customers to start or stop their electric service online.

While setting up our electricity service in Hilo, we had our first experience of "talk story" while waiting in line. The person ahead of us had attended the same high school as the clerk responsible for processing new accounts. Setting up new accounts was put on hold for 20 minutes while they caught up on what all their high school friends were doing. Half way through the 20 minute session, a manager came over and we were certain their presence would bring a quick end to the "talk story" and get the line going again. Instead, the manager joined in the discussion and extended the session for another 10 minutes. When you are waiting in line on Hawaii Island, a "talk story" session will often start. We have become accustom to the delays and wait patiently for the session to end and many times we listen in and find the information exchanged interesting and useful. It is one of the slow lane life styles of living in Hawaii.

There are no natural gas distribution lines on the island. If a house or rental has gas appliances, then they must use propane in tanks.

Solar power is popular due to the high cost of electricity and the state has a law requiring solar water heaters be installed for new houses.

Telephone Services:

Hawaiian Telcom, headquartered in Honolulu, offers telephone services as well as internet and video services. Their service can be set up online or over the phone and they have offices in Hilo and Kona.

Hawaiian Telcom Office in Hilo

Hawaii County is supported by numerous cell companies including Verizon, Sprint, T-Mobile, AT&T, and Mobi PCS.

Cable and Internet Service:

Oceanic Time Warner provides the island cable and internet services. They have a high speed internet service that has met our bandwidth usage needs. They also offer an internet telephone service. Oceanic Time Warner has offices in Hilo and Kona where you have to go to pick up modems and cable boxes.

Oceanic Time Warner Office in Hilo

Trash (Rubbish) Services:

Hawaii County does not provide curb trash service. We paid a local company for weekly trash pickup at our rental house in Hilo. We took excess garbage and green waste to the Hilo landfill. In Kona, trash service was included in the condominium owner's monthly maintenance fee. There are private garbage companies on the island that provide trash pickup services to businesses, condominiums, and individual houses.

Hawaii County has landfills in Hilo and North Kona. The Hilo landfill is located near the Hilo airport at the end of Leilani Street and the West Hawaii landfill in North Kona is located near Waikoloa Beach.

Over twenty county transfer stations are located around the island where residents can take their trash and items to recycle. The transfer stations have chutes to drop in your garbage bags. There are bins for recycling glass, newspapers, and cardboard. Green waste is accepted and on certain days hazardous waste items are collected.

Green Waste at Kona Transfer Station

Security Services:

Theft is the most common crime in Hawaii, so if you are not in a gated community that provides some protection or surveillance for your vehicles and belongings, a home security system is a good idea. Security systems can be a simple burglar alarm or a complex installation of motion detectors and cameras. The prices vary depending upon the complexity of the system and whether the security company responds or an alert is sent to the police.

Licensing Vehicles in Hawaii

You must have Hawaii license plates on your vehicles within 30 days of their arrival in the state. Officials can easily verify compliance with this law by checking the bill of lading issued by the shipping company that transported the vehicle to the island. Out-of-state license plates are very noticeable on an island where all the cars and trucks have license plate numbers that contain an "H", for Hawaii County.

The vehicle registration process in Hawaii County requires that the vehicle first be insured in the state, then pass a state safety inspection, and finally obtain a Hawaii State title and license plates. Even vehicles from another island in Hawaii must be registered in the county they reside.

Auto Insurance:

We visited the auto insurance company that we used on the mainland before our cars arrived on the island. We were hoping that our decades of loyalty with the company would help us get covered, but it did not seem to make any difference in their attitude about taking us on as clients. They were more concerned about where the cars would be parked and how much driving we planned to do. They agreed to insure the cars and our belongings in our rental house as well. Once the cars arrived, they physically inspected our cars and handed us proof of insurance in Hawaii.

Our auto insurance costs in Hilo were about the same as what we paid in Northern California. When we moved to Kona, our auto insurance increased because our cars were parked within a tsunami evacuation zone and we no longer had a garage.

Hawaii Vehicle Safety Inspection sticker

State Safety Inspection Sticker:
With a Hawaii insurance identification card for the vehicle, it is possible to get a Hawaii safety inspection certificate and sticker for the car bumper. Many service stations and car repair shops in Hawaii have signs advertising that they will do a state safety inspection. In addition to checking the car's condition, they verify that your vehicle's registration (from out-of-state if you just arrived on the island) is valid and that the car is

insured in Hawaii. If the car does not pass inspection, then you have to make the repairs to get the certificate.

We used Midas in Hilo and for $15.31 (per car) they gave us a certificate for each car, which we needed in order to get Hawaii titles and license plates. We later returned to Midas with our new Hawaii license plates and they put the new plates on the cars and attached safety stickers to the bumpers.

County of Hawaii Aupuni Center in Hilo

Hawaii Vehicle Title and License:

Hawaii County's Vehicle Registration and Licensing Division offices are located at the Aupuni Center in Hilo, the West Hawaii Civic Center in Kona, and in Pahoa. The offices issue bicycle, motorcycle, moped, and trailer licenses as well.

The Hilo office opens at 8 AM and to avoid a long line we arrived before they opened. By the time we had completed the process to register our two cars, there was a long line of people waiting.

County Vehicle Registration Office Suite 5 in Hilo

Hawaii County has furlough days which usually fall on the first Friday of each month. These cost saving measures close all the Hawaii County offices to reduce the payroll. Hawaii also has some unique holidays like Prince Kuhio day in March and King Kamehameha day in June that close all the state and county offices.

When you go to get a Hawaii car title and license plates, you need to bring the last issued title and registration for the car, a signed bill of lading or receipt from the shipping company, the Hawaii safety inspection certificate, proof of Hawaii auto insurance, a photo id, and money or check to pay the fees.

If the vehicle is new, you need a State of Hawaii form G-27 with any required attachments from the State of Hawaii Department of Taxation. If the weight of your vehicle is not on the title or on other documentation, the county may require the vehicle to be weighed on a state certified scale.

West Hawaii Civic Center in North Kona

The car's registration and safety inspection stickers must be renewed every year. The stickers are color coded and easy for the police to spot when they are out of date.

Getting a Hawaii Driver's License

Hawaii does not require you to get a driver's license if you have a valid license from another state in the United States or other approved license to drive. However, when you get a Hawaii driver's license you must give up any other driver's license.

Hawaii County Police Department in Hilo

If you have a valid driver's license, you only have to pass the written test and a vision test. The Hawaii driver's manual can be found online and is available in many retail outlets on the island. The motorcycle manual is different. The driver's manual has 170 questions in the back and the written test is comprised of a random selection of 30 of them.

The office in Hilo is located at the Hawaii Police Department building, not the Aupuni Center. Driver's license offices are also located in Kona at the West Hawaii Civic Center, Pahoa, and Na'alehu in the Ka'u District.

You can check the Hawaii County website (see References and Resources section at the back) to verify when the offices are open for written tests and for dates of holidays and furlough days.

Unique street signs in Hawaii County

When you go to get a driver's license, you need to bring your valid driver's license, your Social Security card (a photocopy will not be accepted), and money to pay the fee (credit and debit cards are not accepted). If you have changed your

85

name, you have to show proof with a marriage certificate or certified decree of name change.

If you do not have a valid driver's license, you must take the driving test as well as the written test and show proof of your name and date of birth. If you do not have a Social Security card, you must show proof of your legal presence in the United States with immigration papers, resident card, employment authorization, or other acceptable document.

When you arrive at the office, you have to fill out an application with your mailing and actual addresses, your height, weight, and other information. You have the option of registering to vote as a part of the application. After filling out the application you have to stand in line and wait for assistance. When called upon, you are asked for your valid driver's license, which they keep, and your Social Security card. A vision test is given using a machine that checks your eye sight and peripheral vision. If you wear glasses, you can keep them on during the test.

If you pass the vision test, you are given the written test to fill out. When you are finished, your test is graded to verify you have a passing score.

We were surprised at our low scores on the written test. We passed, but just barely. One of the differences as compared to the mainland driver's license tests we have taken is that the questions sometimes require that you pick a response that is the "least wrong" or "most correct", versus a clearly correct answer.

If you pass the test, they accept your payment, take your photo, get your signature, take your finger prints, and hand you a Hawaii driver's license. The day we went in, there were two other people getting a license and it took us over 45 minutes to leave with our license.

Hawaii is strict in their enforcement of seat belts and children being properly secured in approved child passenger restraint systems. The driver is responsible for compliance with seat belt and child car seat laws. Children under four years of age must be secured in approved safety car seats and booster seats are required for children four to seven years of age unless the child is taller than 4'9". Drivers must wear a seat belt and are responsible for all passengers under the age of 15 using their seat belts.

It is illegal in Hawaii to use cell phones or other mobile electronic devices while driving. The legal drinking age is 21 in Hawaii and it is illegal to drive under the influence of an intoxicant. Hawaii County police use marked police vehicles as well as unmarked cars owned by individual police officers with a blue light on the top.

There are signs on the island with "minimum speeds" of 35 miles per hour (MPH) on roads where the maximum speed is 55 MPH. Some drivers are so laid back they drive abnormally slow so the signs are an attempt to make them drive faster. Initially, we found it aggravating to be stuck behind these slowpokes, but now we have to pull over to let impatient tourists get past us. You know you are living in the slow lane when you catch yourself driving 40 MPH in a 55 MPH zone.

Hawaii Police Car with a blue light

Getting a Parking Permit for Disabilities

Hawaii's Department of Health and Safety issues parking permits to allow a vehicle to park in a space reserved for persons with disabilities. The permit is a windshield placard that hangs from the rear view mirror or special license plates that have the international symbol of access. In order to qualify, a doctor who is licensed to practice in Hawaii must certify that you have a mobility impairment. You do not have to be a Hawaii resident to get a placard, but you have to provide proof of your identity along with the doctor's certification. Hawaii allows naturopathic physicians licensed in the state to certify the disability.

Disability Parking Placard

You can apply for a permit at the Office of Aging and Disability Resource Center in Hilo or at the Mayor's office in Kona. The fee for the permit varies depending upon how long the disability is expected to last. A placard for a disability expected to last for at least 6 years is free.

Reserved parking in Hawaii

Hawaii Island has a lot of disabled people perhaps attracted by the island's warm weather. It is common for all of the disabled parking spots to be filled shortly after stores open. Some of our disabled friends fume at the shortage of disabled parking while others just ignore it and take the lack of a parking spot as a sign that it was not the right time to eat at a particular restaurant. The shortage of disabled parking spaces means parking in one of the spots without a placard or license plates will likely result in a parking citation.

Other IDs available in Hawaii

Hawaii issues identification cards that can be used in place of a driver's license to cash checks, travel on an airplane, and get county services. A Hawaii State ID is also used by people who own property or rent long-term on the island but choose to keep an out-of-state driver's license.

Many part-time residents use their Hawaii ID to get discounts at golf courses, hotels, restaurants, and obtain services, known as *kama'aina* rates. In the past they could prove their "residency" with utility bills from their home or rental, even though they maintained an out-of-state driver's license or were not citizens of the United States.

Hawaii has changed their policy and now prints the person's actual residence on the card rather than the address from a local utility bill. If a business or county employee notices the out-of-state address on the Hawaii ID card, they may not give *kama'aina* rates for services and products. Giving false information to obtain a card is punishable by a fine or jail time.

Hawaii State IDs are issued at the Hawaii State building in Hilo and at the Governor's office in Kona. The cost is $15 and you must fill out an application, bring your Social Security card, passport or birth certificate, marriage certificate, and proof of Hawaii residency.

Getting Medical Insurance

Kaiser Offices in Hilo

When we arrived in Hawaii our medical insurance was covered by COBRA (Consolidated Omnibus Budget Reconciliation Act) which gives workers and their families who lose their health benefits when they lose their job the right to continue their group health benefits. Though we did not want an interruption in our health insurance, the cost of COBRA was over $21,000 a year so we were very motivated to find local medical insurance as soon as possible. There are two primary choices for medical insurance on Hawaii Island: HMSA and Kaiser Permanente.

HMSA (Hawaii Medical Services Association) is Blue Cross/Blue Shield for Hawaii and a popular choice for employees of the county, state, and local businesses. HMSA allows you to select your own doctors. Individual HMSA coverage is expensive, so we investigated getting their more affordable catastrophic insurance but they had Hawaii residency requirements that we did not meet at the time.

Kaiser Permanente is a Health Maintenance Organization (HMO) that has their own doctors, medical facilities on the island, and a hospital on Oahu. Kaiser had a reasonably priced family plan and no residency requirements. We were able to apply online and get an estimate, which in our case was $4,000 a year for the family. The price was low because none of us had a pre-existing health condition and the plan limited some medical procedures, like prenatal care. During the five years we have had our Kaiser policy, the cost has more than doubled to over $8,000 a year.

Health care professionals are in short supply on Hawaii Island and many types of specialists and medical tests are not available and require a trip to Oahu. Though Kaiser has a limited number of doctors on the island, they fly specialists in from Oahu for scheduled visits.

Kaiser and HMSA both offer Medicare network and advantage plans on the island. If you choose a catastrophic coverage plan to minimize your costs, there are urgent care facilities and doctors who take cash payment for care.

Hilo Medical Center

Hawaii Island has public hospitals in Hilo, Kohala, Ka'u, and Kona operated by Hawaii Health Systems Corporation (HHSC). HHSC was established by Hawaii State Legislature in 1996 to manage and operate the twelve community-based hospitals in the state. North Hawaii Community Hospital is a private hospital in Waimea.

For serious injuries or illnesses, patients are air lifted to Oahu where the Queens Medical Center is the only major public hospital. Members of Kaiser are sent to the Kaiser Medical Center in Honolulu.

We do not have dental coverage and many people we know pay cash for their dental procedures. They find a dentist they like and work out a payment plan for fillings, root canals, and other dental work.

Though Kaiser has eye checks and glasses available, we have found it less expensive to use the eye doctor and buy glasses and contact lens at COSTCO.

North Hawaii Community Hospital

The lack of specialists and medical facilities has forced many people we know to return to the mainland or travel to Oahu to resolve their health issues. Though the sun, warmth and *aloha* spirit can "cure" a lot of ailments, there are some health problems that require medical care that is not available on the island.

Mail Services on Hawaii Island

Hilo Post Office

Mail service is very important to people living on a remote island. It can take months to get a package sent by ship and even air service is limited. Hawaii Island has no "overnight" service and two days is about the fastest time a package can make it to the island from the mainland.

Federal Express (FedEx) seems to have the fastest service, perhaps because they have an airplane that lands in Hilo and Kona daily. But the United Parcel Service (UPS) and US Postal Service (USPS), which depend on air flights to the island, sometimes surprise us with fast delivery. FedEx and UPS have facilities near the Hilo and Kona airports. In general, mail service is slow and costly to Hawaii Island.

Kona Post Office

If you have an unusual clothing or shoe size, mail order may be the only way to get what you need. However, the cost of shipment can sometimes exceed the cost of the item being ordered. When free shipping is available, it can make a food or clothing item substantially lower in cost than merchandise in local stores.

There are often long lines of people waiting to mail packages at the post offices on Hawaii Island. Hawaii is similar to Asia in the custom of year-round gift giving, called "omiyage". It can take a long time to process forms for packages being sent to Japan and other parts of Asia. Furthermore, many local vendors mail products purchased by tourists to the mainland as a service which adds to the post office traffic.

The downside of mail delivery

The US Post Offices in Hawaii have specially printed priority mail "Aloha boxes" which we use to send gifts. To save time, we use a machine at the Kona Post Office to label packages instead of waiting in line.

US Post Office boxes

Chapter Five
MONEY MATTERS

Lifestyle and your Neighborhood

Condominiums on Hawaii Island

Finding an affordable lifestyle on Hawaii Island can be a challenge even for people who are well off by mainland standards. The island attracts the wealthiest people from around the world to live and vacation. In Hilo, we saw ships in the bay that were so large we assumed they were cruise lines until we found out they were personal yachts. We marvel at the rows of private jets parked at the Kona airport and the onboard helicopter that shuttles a well-known billionaire from his yacht parked in Kailua Bay to his mansion nearby. Though it rarely makes the news, we hear stories about the billionaires and their poorer multi-millionaire friends dining, attending church, and doing other activities when they are on the island.

Alongside the super-wealthy, in some cases within the same communities, there are families on Hawaii Island living at subsistence levels with almost no money. Many workers and retirees have minimum wage jobs or small pensions and rely on food stamps to feed their families. It can be disorienting to live in a place with such extremes in incomes and a challenge to find the right neighborhood.

Houses in Waikoloa Village

We find the logic of Michael Masterson's cost of living model a compelling way to define the cost of a lifestyle in Hawaii. Masterson's model factors in the expenses of a lifestyle from taxes, utilities, insurance, maintenance, clothing, furniture, and keeping up with the neighbors based on the value of the home you are living in. His model predicts that your cost of living will be 40% of the value of your home every year to support the lifestyle that goes along with the home and neighborhood. Yearly expenses are driven by external pressures from neighbors and surrounding businesses that ratchet up prices based on the home values in the neighborhood. Community organizations and social events require expenses on food and clothing. There may be family and social pressures to pay for private schools, cleaning services, house upgrades, gourmet dining, family reunions, car pooling, private lessons, golfing, or club memberships. Homes in upscale neighborhoods have greater lawn care and maintenance costs and some have large monthly maintenance fees to cover utilities and security. Using Masterson's calculation, the lifestyle associated with living in a $200,000 home would cost a family $80,000 a year after taxes, not including any mortgage payment.

Masterson's cost of living model has been an accurate prediction of our annual expenses even though we live in rental homes on the island. For example, living a condominium valued at $320,000 by Hawaii County (with a monthly rent of $1500) predicts yearly expenses of $147,200 after taxes. Over 50% of our annual expenditures are on insurance and college expenses which may seem unrelated, but fall into the model of expected expenses based on lifestyle. Interestingly, as the market valuation of our rental fell over the past two years, so did our cost of living.

The High Cost of Energy in Hawaii

Diesel power plant in Hilo

We knew before moving to Hawaii that electricity was expensive, but we assumed that the high electric bills people complained about were due to them continuously running air conditioners. We had no heaters or air conditioners in Hilo, so the electricity we were using was only for the lights, fans, hot water heater, washer, dryer, refrigerator, stove, and electronics. We were surprised when we received a $450 electricity bill after our first month in Hilo, for the same amount of kilowatt-hours we used in California where we paid only $100 a month.

Since that time we have made it a priority to find as many ways as possible to save on our use of electricity. We have replaced our lights with LED lights, we switch off the water heater when it is not in use, we wash clothes in cold water, we turn off the drying cycle on the dish washer, and we turn off all appliances, fans, and lights when they are not in use. Yet even with all of our cost saving measures, our monthly electric bill is still over $150 for a fraction of the electricity we used on the mainland.

Energy from the wind at South Point Hawaii

Hawaii Island has the largest percentage of electricity generated from renewable sources in the state and the country. Investors were drawn to the island by a state law that made it mandatory for Hawaii's electric utility company, HELCO, to pay oil-based prices for renewable sources of electricity. Investors have built facilities on the island to generate power from geothermal, wind, solar, and hydroelectric to sell to HELCO. The downside of tying HELCO's electric contracts to the price of oil has meant that residents and businesses on Hawaii Island are paying dearly for these lower-cost, renewable forms of energy.

In 2008, the state of Hawaii signed an energy agreement to decouple energy costs from fossil fuel prices for renewable energy contracts, but existing contracts guarantee high returns to investors in Hawaii County for 10 to 15 more years.

Below is one of our monthly residential electric bills from Hawaii Island during 2012 that shows the adjustments and additions charged for electricity:

378 kilowatt hours = $163.92
Customer Charge $10.00
Non-fuel energy (labor and maintenance) $48.28
Base fuel energy $63.30
Interim increase from 2010 $2.12
Public Benefits Fund (pbf) surcharge $2.56
Energy Cost Adjustment $37.66
Overall $.434 per KWH

Fortunately, the cost of solar power systems has dropped over 55% in the last five years, making solar energy a more cost effective option for reducing high electricity bills. Hawaii has a law requiring all new houses to have solar energy hot water systems, which can lower the cost of electricity in the home by up to 40%.

The high cost of electricity increases the cost of water and sewer services. The County Department of Water Supply is the largest customer of HELCO and over a third of the water department's budget goes to pay for the energy costs to pump water around the island.

Solar panels on Hawaii house

Some hobbies and activities are excessively expensive because of the high cost of electricity. Electric kilns for ceramics, foundries for heating metals, bakeries, and computer data centers are rare on the island.

Some people run their air conditioners continuously to keep cool and reduce the humidity. This style of indoor living can mean an extra thousand dollars a month in electricity costs. The high cost of energy on Hawaii Island may change your habits, hobbies, and lifestyle.

Hawaii State Residency and Taxes

Many people who live in Hawaii County are not residents of the state of Hawaii. Some of them own homes in another state or country. Others, however, maintain an address in one of the states in the United States without income tax to avoid having to pay taxes to Hawaii on their retirement or investment incomes.

Hawaii has the highest maximum tax rate in the United States for individuals earning more than $200,000 and couples earning more than $400,000, however, Hawaii has lower rates than some states for lower incomes. For example, individuals earning $48,000 a year in Hawaii are taxed at a rate of 8.25% whereas in California they are taxed at a rate of 9.3% for the same income and individuals earning $125,000 in Oregon are taxed at a rate of 9.9% whereas Hawaii has a tax rate of 8.25% for individuals who earn that income. Hawaii has 12 income brackets with a maximum tax rate of 11%. Couples filing jointly pay a lower overall rate on their combined income. When evaluating a job opportunity in Hawaii, the state's higher income tax should be considered as part of the cost of living on Hawaii Island.

Taxes pay for the critical infrastructure and services that everyone living in Hawaii needs. We were excited to become residents of Hawaii and register to vote. We believe contributing financially to our island community by paying taxes has positive psychological benefits for us.

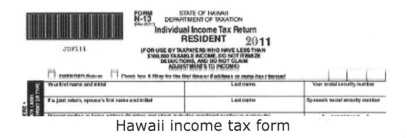
Hawaii income tax form

Only a small percentage of the people who live or own homes in Hawaii County, particularly on the west side of the island, are registered voters. In our Kona condominium complex of 200 units, we could count on one hand the owners who could vote in the last county election. As a result, elections for local offices in Hawaii County are decided by a small number of votes. Ironically, the non-voters are more vocal and more distressed about how the county is run than those of us who vote.

Many people who criticize the decisions made by local elected officials do not fully appreciate the island's unique challenges. For example, the purchase of an island-wide police radio system was extremely expensive in order to get coverage around the complex geological shapes created by the massive volcanoes in the center of the island. Non-residents ranted about corruption in the county because in Oklahoma a radio system would cost less, a lot less.

Voting in Hawaii County elections

Local politics are dominated by being on a remote island with limited services, numerous natural hazards, and the majority of the voters on the east side of the island. Hawaii County officials have limited governance over the island because the governing body in Honolulu controls the state's schools, roads, unions, utilities, harbors, parks, beaches, licenses, and most of the land. The federal government controls another big chunk of the island with national parks and military reservations.

Being a legal resident of Hawaii has benefited us financially. As residents, we get special *kama'aina* prices for hotel rooms, restaurants, and other services on Hawaii Island and in Honolulu. These savings have added up over the years. We have held volunteer positions that are only available to residents with Hawaii driver's licenses. Only residents can run for office or serve on county committees and most jobs require a local driver's license or Hawaii State ID. Hawaii has many services for the sick, poor, young, and elderly and there are special tax breaks that you can receive if you are a resident.

We recommend comparing the costs of maintaining an out-of-state driver's license and address to the lost benefits of being a local resident and having *kama'aina* status. The benefits of being a resident of Hawaii may be worth paying annual income taxes on retirement benefits or investments if you are living full time in Hawaii.

Shopping on Hawaii Island

Shopping for fresh produce on Hawaii is an adventure and delight. If you prefer mainland foods or you live to shop, you may find Hawaii Island shopping a disappointment. We know of many people who left the island over lack of malls and choices in retail merchandise. Stores on Hawaii Island have a limited selection of mainland products and the prices are high because of the cost of shipping or flying them to the island.

Hilo Farmers Market

Hawaii grown food Shopping:
The availability of fruits, vegetables, beef, pork, chicken, and lamb raised on Hawaii Island makes access to healthy foods abundant and affordable.

An incredible array of tropical fruits and vegetables are grown around the island. Farms at the higher elevations of the volcanoes grow

110

lettuce, pumpkins, radishes, and many types of Asian vegetables. The Hamakua Coast is renowned for its tomatoes, cucumbers, and mushrooms. Coconuts, chocolate, avocados, coffee fruits, and macadamia nuts grow around the island. Fruits like bananas and avocados have dozens of varieties that grow on the island and the taste differences are delightfully surprising. If you are adventurous, there are an endless variety of tropical fruits to try.

Grocery store vegetables in Hawaii

Farmer's markets are open around the island almost every day of the year. Neighbors and friends exchange the bounty grown in their backyards and we know of people who drive to public areas and collect fruit on the ground.

Vegetables and fruits must be carefully washed because there are dangerous parasites on the island.

Being knowledgeable about produce from the island and how best to prepare local foods can lower the cost of your food and add new dishes and tastes to your meals.

Every season different varieties of fish and marine life show up in Hawaiian waters and are found in grocery stores and from local fishermen.

Fresh caught fish in Hilo

Hawaii Island ranchers raise grass-fed cattle and local farms raise pigs and chickens. These local meats are available in grocery stores and farmer's markets. Grocery stores and even COSTCO and Target sell fruits and vegetables grown on the island as well as produce from other Hawaiian Islands.

Hawaii Island raised grass fed beef

Any perishable foods that are not produced on the island have to be transported a long distance in refrigerated containers.

Milk shipped from the mainland to Hawaii Island

The shipping costs increase the prices by 25% to 75% and the products are older with a higher probability of being out of date. After repeatedly bringing home moldy bread and spoiled cartons of yogurt and cottage cheese, we now carefully inspect expiration dates.

Occasionally there are eggs available from local farmers, but they do not produce enough for the island. There are goat farms in Puna that make great feta cheeses and there is one small dairy open on the island. The high cost of electricity has made it difficult for bakeries to stay in business, but bread baked in Oahu is flown to Hawaii Island and grocery stores and small bakeries make special occasion breads and sweets.

Grains, beans, oils, potatoes, and some spices are not grown on the island. Rice is the most popular and least expensive grain shipped to the island, but many of us do not want to do without bread.

We do not buy breakfast cereals, pre-packaged meals, chips, crackers, and sauces. For products we must buy like toilet paper, soap, and canned foods, we shop around for the best prices at the big box stores like COSTCO, Target, Wal-Mart, and Safeway. Prices for these types of products commonly vary by over 50% from store to store and month to month depending upon sales and promotions. We watch the prices of the items we need and buy extra when we see a good deal.

COSTCO in North Kona

We buy food and many other products online from Amazon, which offers free shipping for some products to Hawaii through their Amazon Prime program. Free shipping makes the products as cheap as mainland prices and the products are usually fresher.

Buying online allows us to have foods and products that we rarely find in our local stores like wild rice and brown rice pasta. We regularly buy organic flours, oils, almond butter, vitamins, rice, pasta, jam, and powdered egg whites from Amazon. Buying ingredients online reduces the cost of making our own breads, tortillas, and sauces.

Box from Amazon with pasta and flour

Hawaii Island has local grocery stores like KTA, Malama Market, and Foodland as well as mainland stores like Safeway, CVS (Longs) and Walgreens. Target and Wal-Mart sell food at their stores in Kona and Hilo. COSTCO has a store near the Kona airport and COSTULESS has a store in Hilo.

Hawaii Island KTA Superstore in Hilo

Island Naturals (in Hilo, Kona, and Captain Cook) and Abundant Life Natural Foods (in downtown Hilo) sell health foods, food supplements, and vegan items.

Hawaii Island is a cash economy and people go food shopping when they get their paychecks. Many island families receive food stamps so stores are busy the day after the EBT (Electronic Benefit Transfer) cards are refreshed each month. Stores time their sales during the middle of the week and end of the month. Coupon books and fliers are sent in the mail.

Hawaii Shopping coupons in the mail

If you eat local foods, shop for sales, and avoid mainland products whenever possible, you can lower your food expenses. Modifying our diet to consist primarily of local products has made our monthly food expenses much lower than they were in Northern California and the quality, freshness, and taste of the food is far superior.

117

Retail Shopping:

Hawaii Island has many of the same box stores as on the mainland, an indoor mall in Hilo, and strip malls around the island. K-mart, Home Depot, Wal-Mart, Sears, Lowes, GameStop, Radio Shack, Office Max, Sports Authority, Pet Mart, Macy's, ACE hardware, and Ross Dress for Less all have stores on the island with a selection of mainland products.

Prince Kuhio Plaza indoor mall in Hilo

Kona and Hilo have the most stores, but they are almost 100 miles apart on opposite sides of the island. Stores in Waikoloa Beach and Mauna Lani cater to tourists with luxury products such as jewelry, watches, and art. Crafts and unique items can be found at local boutiques, bookstores, and fairs.

When shopping for clothing or shoes, it can be frustrating to not find your size or favorite color after driving a long distance to a store. Many products are not available at all on the island like business suits and evening dresses. People rely on mail order and fly to Honolulu and the mainland to do their shopping.

You can sometimes find great deals on barely used merchandise at garage sales, thrift stores, and rummage sales. We recently bought a formal tuxedo for $6 that someone had donated to a thrift store on the island. Newcomers are always bringing things from the mainland to the island. When they leave, on average within four years, they sell their furniture, bikes, tools, cookware, electronics, and cars.

Boutiques and specialty shops in downtown Hilo

Getting a Job

Hawaii County Band hires musicians

Employment opportunities on Hawaii Island are available in hospitality, government, retail, restaurants, services, and education. Though hotel chains and stores offer jobs online and there are websites for schools and government jobs, many of the jobs are offered only to residents on the island. If you have an expertise, certifications, or bring a business to the island, it may offer you the best jobs and income opportunities.

Hawaii Island has the most telescope observatories in the world and they hire astronomers, engineers, and computer scientists to manage and maintain the telescopes on Mauna Kea. The National Oceanic and Atmospheric Administration (NOAA), United States Department of Agriculture (USDA), and the USGS Hawaiian Volcano Observatory (HVO) have offices and laboratories on the island.

US Federal Building in Hilo

The University of Hawaii campus in Hilo, community colleges, and schools on the island have teaching and administration jobs. Hawaii Island hospitals and clinics are often looking for experienced workers and medical doctors are in short supply on the island. The Energy Laboratory near the Kona airport houses companies in bio-technology, marine food production, and water purification.

Businesses need workers fluent in Japanese, Korean, Chinese, and other Asian languages. Island businesses often advertise for people experienced in electrical installation, construction, truck driving, pesticide spraying, computer repair, landscaping, engine maintenance, and tropical farming.

Institute of Pacific Islands Forestry in Hilo

Local employers are reluctant to hire people who are not living on Hawaii Island because they are often unprepared for living on a remote island.

Newcomers who stay on the island often leave their first job for another better paying job. We have watched a local delivery company repeatedly train a new hire to deliver and stock soft drinks in a store. By the time the training is complete, the person quits for an easier or better paying job. After two years the company still has not been able to retain a worker for longer than a month. High turnover from employees leaving the island or finding a better job is expensive to employers.

Employers are sometimes reluctant to hire workers from the mainland because they are not familiar with the local culture and way of doing things. The majority of the workers on Hawaii Island were born in the Philippines, Japan, Korea, China, or other Pacific Islands. Newcomers are usually unaware of the cultural differences between Asia and the mainland and their remarks and actions often offend co-workers and customers in Hawaii.

Telescopes on Mauna Kea offer jobs

We know people who were in senior positions at chain stores on the mainland that took a demotion to get a position on Hawaii Island. They assumed that the "work ethic" they used to get a top position on the mainland would quickly get them to the top of an organization in Hawaii. They were dismayed when their usual work practices alienated them from management and their coworkers.

The Asian team work ethic and Hawaii *ohana* work values conflict with the American mainland "self made man". It is hard to move to the top of an organization in Hawaii if you offend everyone with culturally insensitive self promotion.

123

Tree climbers are in high demand

Hawaii Island is off the beaten path and not a career centric place. Many workers have more than one job and live with family or other workers to afford the island's high rents with their low wages. Many of the people who live on the island have income from pensions or investments that they earned on the mainland or elsewhere. If your career or making money is important to you, it may not be the right time to move to Hawaii Island.

Cruise ships and hotels in Hawaii have hospitality jobs

Local jobs are advertised by Hawaii recruiters and the local East Hawaii Tribune and West Hawaii Today newspapers. You can search for local jobs on websites like indeed.com or monster.com using the zip code for Kona (96740) or Hilo (96720). More resources for a job search are located in the resources section in the back of this book.

We have seen online ads for positions at Target, Safeway, Wal-Mart, CVS, Home Depot, OfficeMax, Ross Stores, K mart, Sports Authority, PetCo, Macy's, Tommy Bahamas, UPS, Federal Express, Starbucks, McDonalds, Wendy's, Burger King,

Jack in the Box, Bubba Gump Shrimp, Macaroni Grill, Central Pacific Bank, First Hawaiian Bank, Wyndham Worldwide, Hilton Grand Vacations, Sheraton, Fairmont Orchid, Four Seasons, Marriott, Hertz, Avis, Budget, Enterprise, National, Alamo, AT&T, T-Mobile, Verizon, Time Warner, Midas, and Goodyear.

Mainland stores on Hawaii Island

Some newcomers to the island bring their work or business with them. Some are able to maintain connections with remote co-workers through the internet and frequent trips back to the mainland while others struggle with the six hour time difference between the East Coast and Hawaii. We have met newcomers who brought their skills and services to Hawaii Island only to find that the island's small economy could not sustain their business.

Retail and restaurant jobs are available on the island

If you arrive on the island without an income or job lined up, having savings to live for a year or more will offer the time you may need to find the right work environment and income opportunities.

Chapter Six
LIVING ON HAWAII ISLAND

<u>Fun on the Island</u>

Day at the beach in Hawaii

We have found more fun things to do on Hawaii Island than any other place we have lived in the United States. If you are wondering what there is to do after you move to Hawaii Island, here is a list of our favorite festivals, parades, holiday activities, athletic events, science activities, national parks, and ocean activities. There are so many ways to get involved, volunteer, and make friends on Hawaii Island.

Festivals and Shows:

Every season there are festivals and special events around the island. Events and shows are held to celebrate the many cultures on the island. We enjoy slack key guitar and ukulele music festivals, movie festivals, hula events, coffee, chocolate, mango, and avocado festivals, rodeos, and orchid shows. Festivals and shows are a great way to enjoy island life.

Hawaii County fair

In the summer, Buddhist temples on the island invite everyone for O'Bon dances and lantern floating ceremonies honoring the dead. May Day (May 1) is Lei Day in Hawaii and there are hula and lei celebrations in local schools and at county facilities. In June, a state holiday honors King Kamehameha with festivals and parades in Hawi, Hilo, and Kona. Waimea hosts a cherry blossom festival in the spring, a rodeo during Independence Day, and a pumpkin patch festival before Halloween.

Chinese New Year in Hilo

Hilo has a Chinese New Year festival in the winter, Merrie Monarch Hula Festival over Easter, county fair in the summer, and the Black and White Evening Stroll in November. Music and cultural events are held in resorts and performance theaters all year long. Kona hosts coffee, avocado, and chocolate festivals and monthly street fairs.

Holidays:
People in Hawaii love to celebrate holidays and it is easy to get caught up in the fun and excitement. New Year's Eve is celebrated with

fireworks displays. In Hilo the smoke can be so thick you can hardly see through it.

Holiday hula celebration in Kona

Towns around the island celebrate Memorial Day, Independence Day, and Veterans Day with parades. There are dances on Valentine's Day and egg hunts for the children on Easter.

Holiday buffet at Hawaii hotel

Thanksgiving brings sumptuous buffets at resort hotels and though it may be green and warm, there is lots of Christmas spirit on Hawaii Island. There are Christmas tree lightings, Santas, decorations, craft fairs, hula events, carols sung in English and Hawaiian, and parades.

Athletic Events:

Hawaii Island has many athletic competitions including the Ironman world championships, marathons, triathlons, and golf tournaments that attract thousands of athletes. Most athletic events depend on volunteers to support the visiting athletes and have shorter distance fun runs for everyone to participate.

UHH basketball game in Hilo Civic Auditorium

The University of Hawaii at Hilo Vulcans team has sports competitions and the teams appreciate a crowd to cheer them on at their games. Local high schools and little league teams compete at a high level and their games and competitions are fun to attend.

Outrigger canoe paddling is a major sport in Hawaii and the island has competitions in all age groups and hosts local, state, and international competitions. Fishing competitions are also very popular.

Start of triathlon at Kona pier

Walking, running, biking, and swimming events for causes like cancer, animal welfare, and children's health are always looking for volunteers and participants.

Active seniors (Kupuna) performing hula

University and Science Events:

Hawaii Island has international astronomy observatories, the USDA Institute of Pacific Islands Forestry, NOAA Global Monitoring Observatory on Mauna Loa, the USGS Volcano Observatory, and the University of Hawaii which sponsor lectures, classes, and workshops for the public.

'Imiloa Astronomy Center and 3-D planetarium

The international telescope observatories in Hilo and Waimea host seminars and planetarium shows by local and visiting astronomers. Community members staff museums on the island and provide tours to visitors to educate them on natural history, local history, tsunamis, space travel, and marine life. Volunteers also educate visitors about the reefs and turtles at state and county parks and count whales for the marine research center.

NOAA Mokupapapa Discovery Center in Hilo

Dolphin Quest at the Hilton Waikoloa

National Parks:

Hawaii Island has four national parks including the Hawaii Volcanoes National Park, Pu'uhonua o Honaunau National Historical Park, Kaloko-Honokohau National Historical Park and Pu'ukohola National Historical Site as well as a 175-mile National Historic Trail, *Ala Kahakai*, which traverses through hundreds of ancient Hawaiian settlements.

Guided tour in Pu'ukohola National Historical Site

The national parks offer cultural programs and guided walks. The paths and beauty of the parks are something we never get tired of visiting. We buy a yearly national park pass and visit them frequently. Many local residents volunteer for summer park programs, special events, or as docents.

Ocean and Nature Fun:

Boat owners operate snorkeling, scuba, and fishing expeditions for visitors to the island. Island businesses offer visitors zip lines, botanical gardens, lava viewing tours, helicopter flights, horse stables, three-wheel tours, and other activities. Many businesses give discounts to local residents to help support them during their off season times when fewer tourists are on the island.

Scuba certification class

The beaches on Hawaii Island offer year round swimming, surfing, and just lying in the sun on the sand. The snorkeling is fantastic with colorful corals and beautiful reef fish and other marine life. The thrill of seeing a turtle, dolphin, or whale never seems to go away.

Snorkeling in Kona

Buddhist service in Hilo

Community Involvement:

Volunteer fire fighters, Community Emergency Response Teams (CERT), hospitals, police stations, schools, and community centers welcome volunteers. Veterans groups are active on the island and Hilo has a PX on Keaukaha Military Reservation. Senior centers offer many activities and social events.

There are outlets to teach, play music, write, and contribute to the arts on the island. Theaters showcase local and international talent for entertainment and enrichment.

Aloha Theater in South Kona

Although there are so many fun things to do, our favorite activity is lying on the couch under the ceiling fan and napping in the warm tropical weather.

Activities for Kids and Teens

Hawaii Island has sports, fitness, science, arts, and culture programs for young people.

Soccer game on a Hilo Bayfront field

Sports Teams:

Hawaii County has school and other organized teams for baseball, softball, basketball, paddling, soccer, wrestling, tennis, volleyball, and swimming. The county and schools have swimming pools, gymnasiums and fields which are used year-round for sports teams of all ages. On Saturdays, the parks are filled with families laying out huge meals as their children practice or compete with other teams.

Paddling team competition

Little league baseball teams have performed well at the world series and Hawaii Island athletes often receive scholarships in major universities for their athletic abilities. If your child is interested in sports, Hawaii County offers many choices in teams and types of sports.

Fitness:
There are numerous fitness centers, county facilities, as well as YWCA and YMCA classes for children and teens to get exercise and have fun. The county has over 30 centers on the island with gyms, fields, and swimming pool complexes. The county sponsors classes, teams, camps, and certifications in swimming, life saving, tennis, golf, and numerous physical sports and activities. Hawaii County Parks and Recreation Division lists their quarterly events for each facility in newsletters posted to the county website.

Private schools and gyms offer dance, gymnastics, sailing, horseback riding, kendo, fencing, fitness camps, and other types of physical activities for children and teens. Young people have opportunities to engage in ocean activities on the island like surfing, snorkeling, scuba diving, paddling, and fishing. Instruction and competitions are open and children and teens are encouraged to participate.

Hawaii County Kawamoto swim stadium

Science:

Hawaii Island has a large number of scientists working at the international observatories, federal science facilities, National Parks, and University of Hawaii. The scientists, museums, and private donors have created opportunities in science for young people on the island sponsoring summer camps, science fairs, field trips, clubs, and other science programs on the island.

'Imiloa Astronomy Center in Hilo offers after-school and summer programs in addition to their regular planetarium shows, exhibits, and Hawaiian cultural programs. Astronomers at the University of Hawaii and the international observatories support amateur astronomy clubs which provide young people the opportunity to view the stars at the visitor's center on Mauna Kea. Astroday Institute sponsors astronomy events and an annual event to engage children and teens in science.

Keiki Robot Challenge

Volcanoes National Park has a junior ranger program for teens to learn about volcanoes and geology. Astronaut Ellison S. Onizuka Space Center at Kona airport is an educational facility dedicated to teaching students about space flight.

Arts:

Workshops at the East Hawaii Cultural Center in Hilo include Kid's art camp, children's theater workshops, comedy workshops, ukulele instruction, and more. The Hilo Community Players present professional, amateur, and youth theatre. Similar groups for children and teens exist around the island to support and showcase the arts.

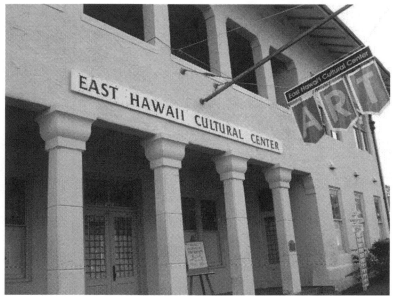

East Hawaii Cultural Center

Libraries on the island offer programs for children during the summer and school breaks. Private schools and the local YMCA, YWCA, and Girls and Boys Club also offer summer programs and activities for children.

Hawaiian Culture:

Hawaiian Hula Schools, *Halau Hula*, are normally founded by a hula teacher who has often inherited the position. The schools teach hula to children and adults and often perform and compete in hula events at hotels and festivals. As a part of their instruction, students learn Hawaiian language, chants, meles, and lei making. Hula is also taught in county recreation programs and at the elementary schools on the island. Publicly funded charter schools offer immersion in the Hawaiian language and culture for children.

Keiki performing hula during Merrie Monarch week

Every spring the Merrie Monarch Hula Festival takes place in Hilo bringing hula groups from around the country to Hawaii Island. Merrie Monarch and numerous other hula festivals and Hawaiian celebrations offer young people the opportunity to participate in hula and Hawaiian culture on the island.

There are many structured and non-structured activities and programs on Hawaii Island that offer children and teens a way to become acclimated to the culture and make friends.

International Pokémon Championships Hilton Waikoloa

Living at a Slower Pace

Being known for your dish at the last pot luck was disorienting for us after decades in the fast-paced business world on the mainland. However, living each day on a warm, tropical island has made it easy to let go of the past and enjoy the here and now.

When we arrived in Hawaii we were obese, stressed, and sluggish. Eating healthy foods, losing weight, and exercising regularly allows us to enjoy the wonderful activities that Hawaii Island has to offer.

Swimming with a turtle

Some people move to Hawaii without realizing their deep connection with relatives and loved ones on the mainland. Travelling back and forth is expensive and stressful. We know many people who moved back to the mainland after deciding they did not want to be so far from their grandchildren or parents.

Keeping in touch with family on Skype

We have noticed that the happy people in Hawaii get along with everyone, treat everyone as an equal, and have a lot of tolerance. They let opinions that bother them roll off their back, they deftly avoid the people who they cannot stand, and they spend their time with people who make them feel happy and upbeat.

People in Hawaii love to "talk story" and there is a wealth of knowledge and experiences that they are willing to share. We sometimes gain a piece of the puzzle of life that allows us to move on emotionally in our life from someone who shares their story with us.

Pot luck with friends in Kona

Every day we find flowers to smell, bird songs to hear, and beautiful scenery to take in on Hawaii Island. Going at a slow pace has allowed us to enjoy and appreciate the beauty and uniqueness of this special island.

GLOSSARY

Living on Hawaii Island requires some knowledge of the Hawaiian language. Most of the street names are Hawaiian names and correct pronunciation is a must in order to understand directions or give an address to get assistance. Below are some Hawaiian and pidgin words commonly heard in local conversations.

a'a – sharp, rough type of lava
ahi – tuna fish
'aina—land, earth
akamai – smart, clever
aku – shipjack tuna fish
Ali'i – royalty, ruling class during the time of Kings and Queens in the Kingdom of Hawaii
aloha - is used to for greetings and describes love or respect for something or someone.
'awa – kava from the black pepper family, a slightly narcotic tea from the root
ha'ole—white person, person of Caucasian descent
hapa—part, fraction, mixed-race, part Hawaiian
hapa-haole or hapa-hula—Hawaiian songs or hula danced to songs (meles) in English
halau –school or group as in a Hula Halau under the leadership of a teacher. It also means long house for canoes.
hale – house
hanai – to feed, adopted

haumana – student

Heiau – ancestral Hawaiian platform temple of worship, *Heiau* ruins can be visited in National and State parks and around Hawaii Island

Hilo – districts in Hawaii County (South Hilo and North Hilo)

hoku – star

holo holo – to go for a walk ride, or sail

honu – green turtle

hui – club, association, society

hula – interpretive dance of Hawaii

huli - The movement of turning over - in a canoe it means to flip over, used to describe chicken roasted on a spit.

humuhumunukunukuapua'a – reef triggerfish that is the Hawaii State fish

imu – underground oven

imua – go forward

kahuna – Hawaiian priest or shaman

kai – sea, area near the sea

Kalakaua – the Kalakaua family were the last rulers of Hawaii Kingdom. King David Kalakaua, also known as the *Merrie Monarch*, took the throne in 1874 and is credited for restoring hula and other cultural traditions to Hawaii. The last ruler of the Kalakaua family was Queen Liliuokalani who was forced to give up her crown when Hawaii became a territory of the United States in 1874.

Kalikimaka – Christmas

kalua – cooked in the ground, kalua pig

kama'aina—native born, now means resident with Hawaii ID or driver's license

Kamehameha – the name of many Kings in Hawaii, King Kamehameha I (1758 – 1819) unified all of the islands of Hawaii and established the Kingdom of Hawaii in 1810. He was born and raised on the island of Hawaii. There is a state holiday for him in June

kane - man and men

kapu—taboo, prohibited, sacred, used on signs to mean "do not trespass"

Ka'u —District in Hawaii County

kea – white, *Mauna Kea* – White Mountain

keiki - child or children, also used to describe the young of anything like banana sprouts are called keiki

koa – a type of wood, fearless

Kohala – districts in Hawaii County (North Kohala and South Kohala)

kokua –help, aid, assist, used on road signs to mean be careful or watch for children and pedestrians

komohana - west

Kona—districts in Hawaii County (North Kona and South Kona), leeward side, winds from the southwest

ko'olau – windward side, north

Kuhio – Prince Jonah Kūhiō Kalaniana'ole Pi'ikoi(1871–1922), also known as Prince Kuhio, was the first Hawaiian native and only royal to serve in Congress. There is a state holiday for Prince Kuhio every March.

kukui - candlenut tree which is the Hawaii State tree

kuleana—right, privilege, responsibility, authority, business, property, estate, portion, jurisdiction, authority, interest, claim, small piece of property

kumu – foundation, teacher who has mastery of Hula or other Hawaiian art form like weaving, they often have a school or following

kupuna – ancestor, elderly person or people

lanai—veranda, patio, or covered porch

Lana'i—island in Hawaii

lani – sky, heaven, heavenly, highborn

laulau – meat wrapped in ti leaves

lei – a garland of flowers, leaves or feathers, May 1st is Lei Day in Hawaii.

liliko'i – passion fruit

loa – distance, height, *Mauna Loa* – Long Mountain

local—person born and raised in Hawaii, not necessarily Hawaiian

lomi – raw salmon, onion and tomato dish

lu'au – feast or celebration with a lot of food

mahalo – thank you

mahimahi – dorado fish

mainland— the continental United States

maka - eye

makai—on the seaside, toward the sea (kai)

make – to die, death, dead

malihini – newcomer to Hawaii, not derogatory

malama—to take care of, tend to, preserve, protect

malama 'aina – take care of and preserve the land

mana – divine power, to have authority

mano – shark

mauka—inland, upland, towards the mountain

mauna - mountain

menehune – legendary race of small people credited for building many of the ancient walls and landmarks

mele - song and poetic language

moku – island, to be cut

mu'umu'u – a loose gown or dress incorrectly called moomoo on the mainland

nani – beauty, glory, pretty

noni – roots and juice of the mulberry tree

nui – big, large, greatest, grand

'ohana – family and extended family, used to describe a standalone housing unit on a property

'okole – behind, the buttocks

oli – chant

ono – delicious, also refers to the Wahoo fish

'opakapaka – red snapper fish

'opihi – limpet

outer islands—or neighbor islands are used to describe all the islands in Hawaii other than Oahu

pahoehoe – refers to the smooth type of lava

pali – cliff, steep hill

paniolo – Hawaiian cowboy

pau – finished, no more, "pau hana" – finished work

Pele – Polynesian goddess of volcanoes and fire

Pele's hair – volcanic glass fibers

pilau – rotten, contaminated

poi – mashed taro root

pono – goodness, righteousness

popolo—African, black person

pule - prayer given in Hawaiian at the beginning of most events on Hawaii Island

Puna—district in Hawaii County, spring (water)

puka – hole, often used to describe a hole in something like a "puka in my pants".

pu'u – hill, mount, lava cone

shaka – Hawaii hand greeting with the thumb and pinky

tsunami—tidal wave (Japanese)

tutu – grandmother, older person. In Hawaii people often refer to their elders as "auntie", "uncle", and tutu

typhoon—hurricane or tropical cyclone (Japanese)

vog—volcanic emissions, from "volcanic smog"

wahine – woman, women

wikiwiki –quick, fast, *wiki wiki* is used to name shuttles and convenience stores

RESOURCES AND REFERENCES

Chapter One

Big Isle Moving and Draying Inc
http://www.bigislemoving.com

East Hawaii Tribune Herald Newspaper
http://www.hawaiitribune-herald.com

Hawaii Island Commercial Harbors
http://www.hawaiiharborsplan.com

Hawaii Volcanoes National Park
http://www.nps.gov/havo

Hilo Farmer's Market
http://hilofarmersmarket.com

Hilo Hawaiian Hotel - A Castle Resort
http://www.castleresorts.com/home/accommodati
ons/hilo-hawaiian-hotel

Hilo Tsunami Map
http://records.co.hawaii.hi.us/weblink/1/doc/339
20/Page1.aspx

Kilauea Lodge in Volcano
http://www.kilauealodge.com

Kona Islander Inn
http://www.konahawaii.com/ii.htm

Matson Navigation
http://www.matson.com

Unipack Global Relocation
http://www.unipack.net

West Hawaii Today Newspaper
http://www.westhawaiitoday.com

Chapter Two

Climate

Juvik, James, et al, *Climate and Water Balance on the Island of Hawaii*, NOAA Mauna Loa Observatory Lab 20th Anniversary Report, pp 129-139, 1978

National Weather Service Forecasts Hawaii:
http://www.prh.noaa.gov/hnl/pages/state_zones.php

Flooding and Tsunamis

Hawaii County Tsunami Evacuation Zone Maps:
http://records.co.hawaii.hi.us/weblink/Browse.aspx?startid=24604&dbid=1

Hawaii Flood Hazard Assessment Tool:
http://gis.hawaiinfip.org/fhat

Japan Tsunami Debris:
http://marinedebris.noaa.gov/tsunamidebris

NOAA Pacific Tsunami Warning Center:
http://ptwc.weather.gov

Lava Zones, Volcanoes, Vog, and Earthquakes

Hawaii County Civil Defense:
http://www.hawaiicounty.gov/civil-defense

Hawaii Department of Health SO2 Advisory:
http://www.hiso2index.info

USGS Earthquake Map (real-time updates):
http://earthquake.usgs.gov/earthquakes/map

USGS Hawaii Island Lava Flow Hazard Zones:
http://hvo.wr.usgs.gov/hazards/lavazones

USGS Hawaii Volcano Observatory Kilauea
Volcano Eruption (real-time cameras):
http://hvo.wr.usgs.gov/cams

Vog Measurement and Prediction Project:
http://mkwc.ifa.hawaii.edu/vmap/hysplit

Vog: State of Hawaii, Important Information:
http://hawaii.gov/gov/vog

Bugs, Frogs, Mold

EHSO, University of Hawaii, *Mold information for the University of Hawaii,* Aug 2010
http://www.hawaii.edu/ehso/mold.htm

Kraus, Fred, *Coqui & greenhouse frogs: alien Caribbean frogs in Hawaii*, HEAR, Feb 2000
http://www.hear.org/AlienSpeciesInHawaii/species/frogs

Rat Lungworm from Hawaii vegetables – what you need to know from Malama o Puna:
http://www.malamaopuna.org/ratlung/needtokno w.php

State of Hawaii Department of Health list of contagious diseases
http://hawaii.gov/health/family-child-health/contagious-disease

Neighborhood Research

Hawaii Business and Contractor license complaints:
http://cms.ehawaii.gov/cms/app/disclaimer.html

Hawaii County Data Book (Census data):
http://records.co.hawaii.hi.us/weblink/Browse.asp x?dbid=1&startid=27952

Hawaii County Environmental Hazards:
http://www.homefacts.com/environmentalhazard s/Hawaii/Hawaii-County.html

Hawaii Criminal Record search:
https://ecrim.ehawaii.gov/ahewa

Hawaii Land and Title Record search:
https://boc.ehawaii.gov/docsearch/nameSearch.h tml;jsessionid=5D8E6847F0F487870BE1DF29A82 86ACD.luka

Hawaii Police Department – Hawaii Island:
http://www.hawaiipolice.com

Hawaii Registered Sex Offender location search:
http://sexoffenders.ehawaii.gov/sexoffender

Hilo Crime Rates:
http://www.neighborhoodscout.com/hi/hilo/crime

UH Hilo Crime Statistics:
http://hilo.hawaii.edu/auxsvc/security/uhhilo.php

Renting in Hawaii

Hawaii Fraud Prevention Resource Guide:
http://hawaii.gov/health/eoa/Docs/Fraud.pdf

Hawaii Property Management Basics Handbook:
http://hawaii.gov/dcca/real/real_ed/re_ed/ce_pre
lic/property_management_basics_handout_-
_final.pdf

Hawaii Residential Landlord-Tenant Code
Handbook:
http://hawaii.gov/dcca/ocp/landlord_tenant/landl
ord-tenant-handbook.pdf

Hawaii State Consumer Protection:
http://hawaii.gov/dcca/ocp

Tropical Home Design

Your Ideal Hawaii Home
http://youridealhawaiihome.com

Chapter Three

Airports on Hawaii Island

Hilo International Airport (ITO)
http://hawaii.gov/ito

Kona International Airport at Keahole (KOA)
http://hawaii.gov/koa

Upolu Airport Hawi
http://hawaii.gov/hawaiiaviation/hawaii-airfields-
airports/hawaii/upolu-airport

Waimea-Kohala Airport (Bordelon Field)
http://hawaii.gov/mue

Hawaii Island Cars Dealers and Service Centers

BMW Hawaii (services BMW)
http://www.bmw-of-kona.com

Big Island Honda (services Honda, Jaguar, and
Land Rovers)
http://www.hilohonda.com

Big Island Motors (services Mazda, Hyundai,
Subaru)
http://www.bigislandmotors.com

Big Island Toyota (services Toyota, Suzuki, Scion)
http://www.bigislandtoyota.com

Kamaaina Motors (Chrysler, Dodge, Jeep, Ram)
http://www.kamaainamotors.net

Kama'aina Nissan (services Nissan)
http://www.kamaainanissan.com

Kelly Blue Book
http://www.kbb.com

Orchid Auto Center (Ford)
http://fordhawaii.dealerconnection.com

RAGS German Auto Club (services Mercedes,
BMW, Porsche, Mini)
http://www.ragsgerman.com

Shipping to Hawaii

FedEx – Shipping to Hawaii
http://www.fedex.com/us/freight/international-
tools/hawaii.html

Horizon Lines Hawaii Services
http://www.horizonlines.com/Ocean-
Services/Hawaii.aspx

Matson – moving household goods
http://www.matson.com/hhg-personal/learn.html

Pasha Hawaii
http://www.pashahawaii.com

UPS Hawaii Zones and Rates
http://www.ups.com/content/us/en/shipping/cost
/zones/alaska_hawaii.html

Moving Pets to Hawaii

Hawaii Animal Quarantine information
http://hawaii.gov/hdoa/ai/aqs/info

Hawaii Department of Agriculture Animal
Quarantine Branch
http://hawaii.gov/hdoa/ai/aqs/aqs

Hawaii Island Humane Society
http://hihs.org

Guns on Hawaii Island

Big Island Trap Club
http://www.shootpita.com/clubs/bitc/index.htm

Hawaii County Trap & Skeet Range
1010 Leilani Street Hilo

Hawaii Gun laws (Hawaii Revised Statutes
references from Honolulu Police Department site)
http://www.honolulupd.org/info/gunlaw.htm

Keaukaha Military Reservation Rifle & Pistol
Shooting Club
1046 Leilani Street Hilo

West Hawaii Puu Anahulu Public Shooting –
(proposed):
http://www.hawaii247.com/2012/05/23/public-
scoping-meeting-for-puu-anahulu-shooting-
range-june-6

TSA - Traveling with guns
http://www.tsa.gov/travelers/airtravel/assistant/editorial_1666.shtm

Island Banks and Credit Unions

American Savings Bank
http://asbhawaii.com

Bank of Hawaii
http//:www.boh.com

Big Island Federal Credit Union
https://www.bigislandfcu.com

Central Pacific Bank
http://centralpacificbank.com

CU Hawaii Federal Credit Union
http://cuhawaii.com

First Hawaiian Bank
http://www.fhb.com

Hawaii Community Federal Credit Union
http://www.hicommfcu.com

Hawaii County Federal Credit Union
http://hawaiicountyfcu.com

Hawaii Credit Union League
www.hcul.org

Hawaii National Bank
http://www.hawaiinational.com

HFS Federal Credit Union
http://www.hfsfcu.org

HomeStreet Bank
http://www.homestreet.com

Independent Employers Group Federal Credit
Union http://www.iegfcu.com

Territorial Savings Bank
http://territorialsavings.net

Schools on Hawaii Island

Adult Education School - Hilo
http://165.248.6.166/data/school.asp?schoolcode
=483

Adult Education School – Kona
http://165.248.6.166/data/school.asp?schoolcode
=484

Hawaii Community College
http://www.hawcc.hawaii.edu

Hawaii GED program
http://doe.k12.hi.us/communityschools/diplomag
ed.htm

Hawaii Homeschooling
http://homeschooling.gomilpitas.com/regional/Ha
waii.htm

Hawaii Homeschooling - Department of Education
http://doe.k12.hi.us/myschool/homeschool

Hawaii Public Education – article Civilbeat
http://www.civilbeat.com/articles/2011/06/07/11
422-getting-to-the-bottom-of-hawaiis-education-
budget

Hawaii Public Schools
http://doe.k12.hi.us/index.html

Hawaii State Teachers Association (HSTA)
http://www.hsta.org

Private Schools report
http://schools.privateschoolsreport.com/Hawaii/H
I.html

School Ratings
http://www.greatschools.org

University of Hawaii Center – West Hawaii
http://hawaii.hawaii.edu/ucwh

University of Hawaii, Hilo
http://hilo.hawaii.edu

Chapter Four

Sewer Service

EPA Cesspool compliance requirements:
http://www.epa.gov/region9/water/groundwater/
uic-hicesspools.html

Hawaii County Department of Environmental Management, Wastewater Division offices:
Hilo: 2100 Kanoelehua Avenue, C-5 (next to Checkers Auto Parts in the Puainako Town Center)
Kona: 74-5044 Ane Keohokalole Highway Bld D

Hawaii County Sewer Network Maps
http://records.co.hawaii.hi.us/weblink/Browse.aspx?dbid=1&startid=24662

Hawaii County Waste Water Division
http://www.hawaiicounty.gov/dem-wastewater-division

Water

Hawaii County Department of Water Supply
Hilo: 345 Kekuanaoa Street Suite 20
Waimea: 65-1234 Opelo Road
Kona: 78-6717 Mamalahoa Hwy
Ka'u: 95-6041 Mamalahoa Hwy

Hawaii County Water Supply
http://www.hawaiidws.org

Hawaii Drought Monitor: Commission on Water Resource Management
http://hawaii.gov/dlnr/drought/forecast.htm

Macomber, Patricia, *Guidelines on Rainwater Catchment Systems for Hawaii*, University of Hawaii at Manoa, College of Tropical Agriculture and Human Resources, 2010
http://www.ctahr.hawaii.edu/oc/freepubs/pdf/RM-12.pdf

Electric Services on Hawaii Island

HELCO offices:
  Hilo: 1200 Kilauea Avenue
  Kona: 74-5519 Kaiwi Street
  Waimea: HELCO Baseyard

HELCO website:
http://www.helcohi.com/portal/site/helco

Communication Services

AT&T cell service
http://www.att.com

Hawaiian Telcom: land, wireless, and internet
http://www.hawaiiantel.com

Mobi PCS cell and internet service
http://www.mobipcs.com

Oceanic Time Warner offices:
  Hilo: 548 Kanoelehua Avenue
  Kona: 73-4876 Kanalani Street

Oceanic Time Warner website:
http://www.oceanic.com

Sprint cell service
http://www.sprint.com

T-Mobile cell service
http://www.t-mobile.com

Verizon cell service
http://www.verizon.com

Trash Services for Hawaii County

Hawaii County Landfill locations
   Hilo: near the Hilo airport at the end of Leilani Street. To get there, turn toward the airport on Leilani from Highway 11 and follow the street until you see the sign.
   North Kona : Puuanahulu Landfill Road off the Queen Kaahumanu Highway, south of Waikoloa Beach Drive.

Hawaii County Green Waste
http://www.hawaiizerowaste.org/recycle/greenwa
ste

Hawaii County Solid Waste Transfer Stations
http://www.hawaiizerowaste.org/facilities

Hawaii Recycling
http://www.recyclehawaii.org

Vehicle Registration and Licensing

Hawaii County's Vehicle Registration and Licensing Division offices:
   Hilo: Aupuni Center at 101 Pauahi Street. The office is in Suite 5, on the left side of the main entrance
   Kona: West Hawaii Civic Center at 74-5044 Ane Keohokalole Highway
   Pahoa: 15-2615 Keaau-Pahoa Road

Hawaii County's Vehicle Registration and Licensing Division
http://www.hawaiicounty.gov/vehicle-registration-licensing

Hawaii State Auto Insurance Premium Comparison
http://hawaii.gov/dcca/ins/consumer/consumer_i
nformation/mv_premiums

Hawaii Periodic Motor Vehicle Inspection Manual
http://hawaii.gov/dot/highways/admin-
rules/PMVI%20Manual%20for%20Inspectors%20
of%20Pass%20Cars%20.pdf

Hawaii State Driver's License

Hawaii County Department of Finance
http://www.hawaiicounty.gov/finance-dl-general-
information

Hawaii Island Driver Licensing offices
   Hilo: Police Department building at 349
Kapiolani Street, (not the Aupuni Center)
   Kona: West Hawaii Civic Center at 74-5044
Ane Keohokalole Hwy
   Waimea: 67-5185 Kamamalu Street
   Pahoa: 15-2615 Kea'au-Pahoa Road
   Na'alehu: 95-5355 Mamalahoa Hwy

Hawaii Seat Belt Laws
http://www.capitol.hawaii.gov/hrscurrent/vol05_C
h0261-0319/HRS0291/HRS_0291-
0011_0006.htm

Hawaii State Driver's Manual
http://hawaii.gov/dot/highways/hwy-v/A-
HawaiiDriversManual201205.pdf

Permits and IDs

Disability Parking Permit - applying
  Hilo: Office of Aging and Disability Resource
Center at 1055 Kinoole Street
  Kona: West Hawaii Civic Center at 74-5044 Ane
Keohokalole Hwy

Hawaii Health Department Parking Permit rules
http://hawaii.gov/health/dcab/obtainparkingpermi
t

Hawaii Keiki ID Kit
http://hawaii.gov/ag/mcch/main/keiki_id

Hawaii State ID Cards - Applying
  Hilo: Hawaii State Building at 75 Aupuni St.
  Kona: Governor's Office at 75-5722 Kuakini
Highway Kuakini Tower, #215

Hawaii State ID Card information
http://hawaii.gov/ag/hcjdc/main/hawaii_id_cards

Hawaii Island Medical Resources and Insurance

Hawaii Health Insurance Program (SAGE Plus)
http://www.hawaiiship.org

Hawaii Health Services Corporation (HHSC)
http://www.hhsc.org

Hawaii Insurance Consumer Watch
www.hawaii.gov/dcca/ins

Hawaii Medical Service Association (HMSA)
http://www.hmsa.com

Hawaii Medicare Assistance
http://hawaii.gov/health/eoa/SAGEP.html

Kaiser Permanente
http://kp.org

North Hawaii Community Hospital
http://www.nhch.com

Urgent Care - Keauhou
http://www.keauhouvillageshops.com/village-merchants/#Urgent

Urgent Care - Kona
http://www.hualalaiurgentcare.com

Hawaii Island Mail Services

Hawaii Island Post Offices (zip code areas)
96704 Captain Cook
96710 Hakalau
96718 Hawaii National Park
96719 Hawi
96720 Hilo
96721 Hilo PO Boxes
96725 Holualoa
96726 Honaunau
96727 Honoka'a
96728 Honomu
96737 Oceanview
96738 Waikoloa
96739 Keauhou
96740 Kailua-Kona

96743 Kamuela (Waimea)
96745 Kailua-Kona PO Boxes
96749 Kea'au
96750 Kealakekua
96755 Kapa'au
96760 Kurtistown
96764 Laupahoehoe
96771 Mountain View
96772 Na'alehu
96773 Ninole
96774 Ookala
96775 Paauhau
96776 Pa'auilo
96777 Pahala
96778 Pahoa
96780 Papaaloa
96781 Papa'ikou
96783 Peepeekeo
96785 Volcano

Federal Express (FedEx) Offices
   Hilo: FedEx is on the opposite side of the Hilo airport runway from the terminal, accessible from Highway 11 via Operations Road.
   Kona: the FedEx office is at the airport on Uu Street

United Parcel Service (UPS) Offices
   Hilo UPS office is on the road to the airport
   Kona: UPS has a Customer Center at the Kona airport and a UPS Store at 75-5560 Kopiko Street

Chapter Five

Life style calculator from Michael Masterson's logic
http://www.calculatedliving.com/LifestyleCalculat
or.html

Energy in Hawaii

Hawaii Electric Company, Residential Rates
http://www.heco.com

Hawaii State Energy programs:
http://energy.hawaii.gov/programs

Taxes in Hawaii

Hawaii County Real Property Tax and TMK maps
http://www.hawaiicounty.gov/rpt-tmk-sub

Hawaii Income Tax brackets
http://www.bankrate.com/finance/taxes/state-
taxes-hawaii.aspx

Hawaii Individual Taxes Rates 2012
http://www.taxfoundation.org/taxdata/show/228.
html

Politics and Voting in Hawaii County

Guide to Government in Hawaii
http://www.state.hi.us/lrb/gd/gdgovhi.pdf

Hawaii County Council
http://www.hawaiicounty.gov/lb-council-home

Hawaii County Elections Division and Voter
Information
http://www.hawaiicounty.gov/elections-voter-info

Hawaii County Mayor's Office
http://www.hawaiicounty.gov/office-of-the-mayor

Shopping on Hawaii Island

Abundant Life Natural Foods
http://www.abundantlifenaturalfoods.com

Amazon Prime Program
http://www.amazon.com/gp/prime

Big Island Farmer's Markets
http://hawaii.gov/hdoa/add/farmers-market-in-
hawaii/Farmers%20Market%20Listing%201-10-
2011-Big%20Island.pdf

COSTULESS
http://www.costuless.com

Foodland (also Sack N Save, Malama Market)
http://www.foodland.com

Hawaii EBT (Food Stamps)
http://hawaii.gov/dhs/self-sufficiency/benefit/EBT

Hilo Farmer's Market
http://hilofarmersmarket.com

Island Naturals
http://www.islandnaturals.com

Keauhou Shopping Center
http://www.keauhouvillageshops.com

Kings Shops – Waikoloa Beach
http://www.kingsshops.com

Kona Coast Shopping Center
http://www.konashopping.com

Kona Commons
http://www.konacommons.com

KTA Mountain Apple Brand
http://www.ktasuperstores.com/mountainapplebr
and.asp

Parker Ranch
http://parkerranch.com

Prince Kuhio Plaza Mall
http://www.princekuhioplaza.com

Puainako Center Hilo
http://www.puainakocenter.com

Shops at Mauna Lani
http://www.shopsatmaunalani.com

Slow Food Hawaii
http://slowfoodhawaii.org

Suisan Fish Company
http://www.suisan.com

Queens Market Place – Waikoloa Beach
http://www.queensmarketplace.net

Job Search in Hawaii

Employment Search – Hawaii County
http://hiloliving.com/Hilo_Income.html

Hawaii County Jobs
http://agency.governmentjobs.com/countyhawaii/
default.cfm

Hawaii Department of Education Jobs
http://doe.k12.hi.us/personnel/index.htm

Hawaii Health Systems Corporation Jobs
http://www.hhsc.org/recruit/Employment_Section
.htm

Hawaii State Jobs
http://agency.governmentjobs.com/hawaii/defaul
t.cfm

Hawaii State Jobs portal:
http://portal.ehawaii.gov/employment/search-for-
jobs.html

University of Hawaii System Jobs
http://www.pers.hawaii.edu/wuh

University of Hawaii Salaries - civil beat article
http://www.civilbeat.com/articles/2011/11/22/13
930-hawaii-state-salaries-2012-university-of-
hawaii

Chapter Six

Island Activities

Aloha Theater in South Kona
http://www.apachawaii.org

Big Island Cross Fit – boot camps, kids programs
http://www.crossfitbigisland.com

Camping on Hawaii Island
https://www.ehawaii.gov/Hawaii_County/camping

Canoe Clubs in Hawaii
http://www.y2kanu.com/links.htm

Dolphin Research Center – Kula Nai'a
http://www.kulanaia.org

Dolphin Quest – Hilton Hotel
http://www.hiltonwaikoloavillage.com/resort_acti
vities/dolphin_quest.cfm

East Hawaii Cultural Center – workshops
http://www.ehcc.org

Hawaii County Community Emergency Response
Teams (CERT)
http://www.hawaiicounty.gov/civil-defense-cert

Hawaii County Swimming pools
http://www.hawaiicounty.gov/pr-aquatics

Hawaii Island Events
http://www.gohawaii.com/big-island/plan-a-trip/events

Hawaii State Volunteering portal:
http://portal.ehawaii.gov/employment/volunteering.html

Hawaii Volcanoes National Park – volunteer program
http://hvnp.org

Hilo Events Calendar
http://hiloliving.com/Hilo_Calendar.html

Hilo Orchid Society
http://www.hiloorchidsociety.org

Hilo Palace Theater – local and national talent
http://www.hilopalace.com

Learn Hawaiian –Kamehameha School
http://ksdl.ksbe.edu/kulaiwi

Lyman Museum and Mission House
http://www.lymanmuseum.org

Mauna Kea Visitors Center – Astronomy Activities
http://www.ifa.hawaii.edu/info/vis

Merrie Monarch Hula Festival
http://www.merriemonarch.com

NOAA Mokupāpapa Discovery Center -Hilo:
http://www.papahanaumokuakea.gov/education/center.html

National Parks in Hawaii
http://www.nps.gov/state/hi

Pacific Tsunami Museum
http://www.tsunami.org

Planetarium Shows at 'Imiloa Astronomy Center
http://imiloahawaii.org

University of Hawaii Athletic Events
http://hiloathletics.com

University of Hawaii Events
http://www.uhh.hawaii.edu/news

University of Hawaii Hilo Performing Arts Center
http://artscenter.uhh.hawaii.edu

Volcano Art Center
http://www.volcanoartcenter.org

Waimea Community Theater
http://www.waimeacommunitytheatre.org

Kids Activities and Programs

Boys and Girls Club Hawaii
http://www.bgch.com

Halau Hula (Hula Schools)
http://mele.com

Hawaii County Parks and Recreation Dept
http://www.hawaiicounty.gov/parks-and-recreation

Hawaii County Park and Recreation Centers
Program Guides
http://records.co.hawaii.hi.us/Weblink8/browse.a
spx?dbid=1&startid=56280

Hawaii Public Libraries
http://www.publiclibrary.ws/county/Hawaii.html

Hawaii Sports Portal
http://www.hawaiisportspage.com

Junior Ranger Program – National Parks
http://www.nps.gov/learn/juniorranger.cfm

YMCA Hawaii Island
http://www.ymca.net/y-profile/?assn=1519

YWCA Hawaii Island
http://www.ywcahawaiiisland.org

Military Resources on Hawaii Island

Hawaii Office of Veterans Services
http://hawaii.gov/dod/ovs

Hilo Vet Center
http://www2.va.gov/directory/guide

Keaukaha Military Reservation (KMR) – Hilo
Army National Guard
http://hawaii.gov/pwd/rotating-
headlines/keaukaha

Kilauea Military Camp - Volcano
http://www.kmc-volcano.com

KMR Army/Air Force Exchange Service PX
Bldg 505, 1300 Kekuanaua Hilo

Pohakuloa Training Area (PTA) – Saddle Road
http://www.garrison.hawaii.army.mil/pta

UHH Veterans Benefits – GI Bill
http://hilo.hawaii.edu/registrar/veteran.php

VA Outpatient Clinic – Hilo
http://www.hawaii.va.gov/visitors/hilo_cboc.asp

VFW posts in Hawaii
http://www.vfwhawaii.org

Yukio Okutsu State Veterans Home –Hilo
http://www.avalonhci.com/yukio_okutsu_state_v
eterans_home.html

INDEX

Acknowledgements

We want to acknowledge the hundreds of people who emailed us questions about moving to Hawaii over the past five years. Their questions, frustrations, and challenges are the basis of this book. We thank the many people who moved to Hawaii and shared their stories and experiences with us. They helped us focus on the common aggravations that people new to Hawaii struggle with the most during and after their move to Hawaii.

We thank our son, Daniel, for his constant encouragement and enthusiasm while we were writing this book. We also want to acknowledge our parents, Jackie, Tish, and David for reading our last book and giving us great feedback.

We thank our friends Bob and Kim, Bob and Marilyn, Bill and Lois, and Bill and Shirley for their friendship, their support of our book writing, and all the fun pot lucks. We thank the owners of Kona Stories book store in Keauhou, Brenda Eng and Joy Vogelgesang, for their support of us and other authors on Hawaii Island. We are very grateful to Lois Hodges for taking time to proofread our draft and offer us helpful comments.

About the Authors

Tyler and Chris Mercier moved to Hilo to replace their fast-paced life in Silicon Valley with a laid-back, tropical life on Hawaii Island. Since 2007, they have lived in Hilo, Kailua-Kona, and Kamuela where they experienced living in different homes, communities, and climate zones on the island. Tyler and Chris write books, blogs, and websites about homes, health, local foods, and lifestyles on Hawaii Island.

The Mercier's blog at hiloliving.blogspot.com
Their websites are:
hiloliving.com
funhawaiitravel.com
calculatedliving.com.

Other books by Tyler and Chris Mercier:
Your Ideal Hawaii Home: Avoid Disaster when Buying or Building in Hawaii -
published in 2011

Online resources about moving and property ownership in Hawaii are located at YourIdealHawaiiHome.com.

The authors can be contacted at youridealhawaii@gmail.com

Made in the USA
Las Vegas, NV
16 November 2020

10982146R00109